Close to the Edge –
Tales from the Holderness Coast

Sheila Williams

Close to the Edge – Tales from the Holderness Coast

ISBN-13:
978-1514255537

Published: August 2015

For more about the author, visit
writeonthebeach.wordpress.com

CONTENTS

List of Illustrations

Map of the Holderness Coast adapted from Thomas Sheppard's *The Lost Towns of the Yorkshire Coast,* 1912

Cliff Erosion at Aldbrough, © June Berridge

Skipsea Castle today, © June Berridge

1780 caricature of a pressgang

The ruins of Nunkeeling Priory Chapel, © June Berridge

Hornsea Mere, © June Berridge

The Bayle Gate, Bridlington Priory, © June Berridge

Flamborough North Landing, © Sheila Williams

Climmers Going Over the Cliff from *The Birds of Yorkshire* by T H Nelson

Gathering cobbles at Atwick. Photo courtesy Hornsea Civic Society

Revenue cutter chasing a smuggling lugger by Charles Dixon RI (1872-1934)

Joiner's Shop in Mappleton showing nameplates of lost ships. Courtesy Hornsea Civic Society

Figurehead of the *Earl of Beaconsfield*, © June Berridge with permission from Hull Museum

Spurn Lighthouse, © June Berridge

The First Flamborough Lighthouse, © June Berridge

Withernsea Lighthouse, © June Berridge

Wilsthorpe Sands, © June Berridge

The *Serapis* By Robert Dodd (1748–1815),

Pastel portrait of Thomas Grimston reviewing his troops by Henry Singleton c 1794

Ruins of Fort Godwin, Kilnsea, © June Berridge

Kilnsea Sound Mirror – attributed to Paul Glazzard

Study at a Quiet French Watering Place, *Punch* 1877 by George du Maurier,

Hornsea Promenade and Pier Remains, pre-1906. Photo courtesy Hornsea Civic Society

Withernsea Pier; ©June Berridge

Erosion Map showing the Lost Villages, adapted from Thomas Sheppard's *The Lost Towns of the Yorkshire Coast,* 1912

Gravestones in Rimswell Churchyard; ©June Berridge

The Binks and possible site of Ravenser Odd, ©June Berridge

Author's Foreword and Acknowledgements

I came to live on the Holderness coast more by accident than design. I was selling my house in Lincolnshire and after two years waiting for a buyer to come along, I received an unexpected offer for it which prodded me into starting a serious search for a replacement. I had not planned to live on the East coast of Yorkshire, although the idea of coastal living always appealed. However driving along the coast road one day after a visit to a friend in Beverley, I stopped for petrol in a little village and noticed a signpost, 'Viewpoint'. Curious, I followed the sign, parked my car in the clifftop car park and took a deep breath as I looked out over a huge grey-blue sea that transformed itself seamlessly into the sky so it was hard to know where one began and the other finished.

I took a long walk on the beach below. Despite the late summer sunshine there were only a few fishermen and a couple of families packing up after a day out on the sands. The beach was like no other I'd ever seen. There was none of the usual briny scent in the air; there was neither seaweed nor rock pools, just a vast expanse of sand and cobbles. Large round globs of muddy clay peppered with pebbles littered the beach. They reminded me of the eggs in the creature's nest in the film *Alien*. This was my first introduction to the realities of erosion.

Later, after I bought the tatty old school house in the village I began to explore the coastline, where my erosion education expanded as I found roads that dropped off the cliff edge, remains of buildings and structures unceremoniously tipped over onto the beach below and I learned of the villages that had 'gone back to the sea' – some that vanished centuries ago and some in living memory. All this fired my imagination. What was it like living on this coastline with this constant threat? What sort of people lived here and what did they do? How did they manage? Did the erosion concern them or was it something that they accepted as part of their life? So, with my friend and photographer June Berridge, a notebook and camera, we travelled the coastline looking, listening and learning about life at the edge.

If you are looking for a definitive history of the Holderness coast then this book is not it! Fans of strait-laced history too, will need to look for more academic tomes. Rather this book is an eclectic and sometimes irreverent collection of stories about people, places and events relating to this changing coast – chosen for no other reason than they tickled my imagination. I have looked at the past through modern eyes; subjectivity and opinion have crept in and my interpretation of attitudes, motives, behaviours and events provides only one of several possibilities.

Above all though, I hope the book transmits some of the affection I have developed for a part of England where no major event of national importance ever occurred – give or take a couple of landings on the shore by would-be kings who did not pause long to say hello to their future subjects – where the one constant is a hungry sea gnawing at the cliffs; where, over the centuries, people learned to adapt, to build their settlements anew or go under, and where a big sky suddenly shifts from grey, melancholy and brooding to glorious sunlight casting sparklers on the sea.

I have been fortunate in receiving a great deal of help and support whilst writing this book and I have some particular acknowledgements I would like to make.

First to my friend and photographer June Berridge who tirelessly trudged up and down the coast with me, taking photo after photo just to get the shot right whilst I sat on a rock whining about the cold. Thanks Junie.

Next my thanks to Caroline High, my editor, who whipped the book into shape and dealt sympathetically but firmly with all my neuroses and uncertainties.

Then there are the wonderful staff at Bridlington and Hornsea libraries who managed my endless enquiries with great patience; the volunteers at Hornsea Museum and the Lighthouse Museum in Withernsea who shared their knowledge freely; and Hornsea Civic Society who allowed me to plunder its stock of photographs. Thank you all.

Inevitably, I have made a great deal of use of the internet in my research and I have made every effort to source copyright on all quotes and images but information on any oversight would be welcomed and rectified.

Sheila Williams

France, 2015

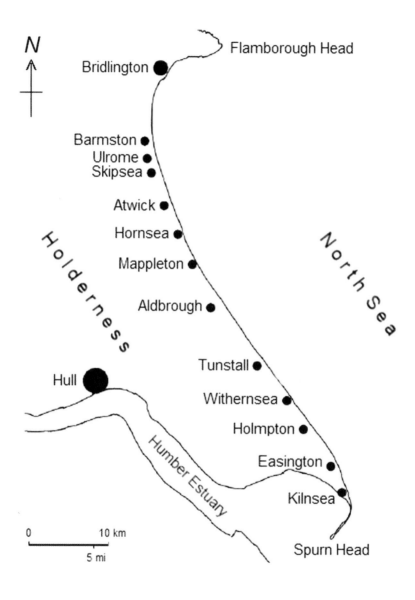

Map of the Holderness Coast, East Yorkshire

Chapter One
Growing Pains

'... the most that I find remarkable here, is, that there is nothing remarkable upon this side for above thirty miles together; not a port, not a gentleman's seat, not a town of note; Bridlington or Burlington is the only place, and that is of no note, only for a bay or road for shipping, which is of use to the colliers on this coast to defend them, in case of extremity of weather.'

Thus Daniel Defoe dismissed the Holderness coast in his book *A Tour Through the Whole Island of Great Britain* which was published in the early 18th century. Perhaps he had supped on bad ale and passed a sleepless night in some bug-infested hostelry which made him particularly grouchy or perhaps he was not looking in the right places. For starters, the geography and geology of the coastline are pretty remarkable in themselves.

WHERE THE WIND WHISTLES

Holderness is part of the East Riding of Yorkshire or East Yorkshire if you want to be pedantically correct. It is a triangular wedge of land running south from Flamborough Head to Kilnsea and Spurn Point. To the north and west it is hemmed in by the rolling Yorkshire Wolds, to the south by the estuary of the river Humber and finally to the east by the encroaching North Sea.

Along the Holderness coast are three small towns – Bridlington, which is the largest, Hornsea and Withernsea – together with numerous villages. This book is concerned with life and events along this coastline – life at the edge – where the sea eats away at the land and has done so almost since the land was formed. So what makes this coast remarkable?

Prior to the last Ice Age two million years ago the coastline consisted of a chalk cliff that stretched from Flamborough down to the town of Beverley and on to Hessle, just west of Hull. The North Sea was relatively dry, known as Doggerland and linked the UK to the rest of Europe. The Holderness coast, indeed inland Holderness too, was a soggy, boggy stretch with meres, creeks and inlets all intermingled with 'carrs' – wet woodland and brush. The whole provided a useful area for the hunting and fishing folk of the Stone and Bronze ages and nothing much more.

As the climate changed the ice retreated, ice sheets melted, water levels rose and the North Sea started to fill. Doggerland disappeared under the waters to become the Dogger Bank. Where they melted, the ice sheets dumped loads of silt, boulders and gravel which formed the cliffs of the coast – cliffs that are soft, unstable and subject to the whims of sea and rain. The one gnaws away at the base of the cliff and the other turns the clay into a gloopy substance – something akin to melted chocolate. The outcome is that the cliffs slump, sag and slide on to the beach below.

Nothing is wasted though; the deposits are washed away down the coast and fetch up further south to create, shape and reshape the Spurn Peninsula, although after the 2013 storm surges Spurn is effectively now more or less an island only accessible on foot. Today the Holderness coast has the dubious honour of being the fastest disappearing coastline in Europe.

Squeezed in with the material dumped by the ice sheets were fossils from the Jurassic Age and other periods, and the regular cliff falls along the coast always reveal a fine selection. Sadly there is no walking with dinosaurs on this coast but rather we may find ourselves treading on the somewhat sinister-named Devil's Toenail (nothing more scary than a common-or-garden fossilised oyster) or waggling the more virtuous St Peter's Fingers (belemnites –related to the modern-day squid).

Cliff erosion at Aldbrough

THE EARLY SETTLERS

However, to return to our story – as the climate improved and an uneasy boundary between sea and land developed, the early hunter-gatherers decided to put down roots and small settlements developed. On the northern end of the coast around Barmston, Ulrome and Skipsea three sites have yielded evidence of use or occupation. Goodies dug up from these sites included axes, spearheads and pottery, as well as some amber and jet jewellery. From bones found in these sites, it appears that the diet of our Bronze Age ancestors included liberal helpings of well-roasted ox -–perhaps laying the foundations of the claim that the English are a nation of beef-eaters. Maybe Yorkshire Pudding followed later?

Possibly the most interesting feature from this time is the inappropriately named Dane's Dyke (it actually has Bronze Age origins) which runs north-south for about two miles across Flamborough Head effectively cutting off the seaward side of the headland. The Dyke is a whopping great bank and ditch earthwork which, even allowing for a bit of assistance from the natural landscape, must have taken who-knows-how-many weeks of backbreaking labour to dig. No Bronze Age JCBs to help out with this little bit of civil engineering. It certainly makes for a superbly defended enclave in the area behind it, with the cliffs to the north, south and east forming a natural barrier. The puzzle is really whether it was created to keep people in or out? There have been no findings of any settlement within the area defended by Dane's Dyke but, on the other hand who or what was being kept out? Some invading force? The jury is still in session.

However, scuttling on a few squillion years, by the Iron Age virtually the whole of the East Yorkshire was part of the kingdom of a tribe known as Parisi. Within the tribe an elite of horsemen and charioteers existed whose power and wealth derived from the possession of horses and cattle. These Iron Age folk had not much to do save hunt, fish, farm and squabble amongst themselves until the Romans came a-calling in AD43 and things began to look up... but not a lot.

The sea and coast held little charm for the Romans who preferred to create towns, garrisons and 'des res' villas inland on the more valuable Yorkshire Wold land. However, they did erect a stone signal tower at Flamborough as part of their early warning system in case of attack and there is evidence to indicate that they built a road along the coastline. Some Italian influences did filter through to the larger coastal settlements such as Bridlington, Hornsea, Aldbrough and Withernsea, as well as to some of the significant strategic places such as Spurn but the Roman style, sophistication and comforts we know and love – baths, central heating, watertight roofs and damp-proof floors – for the most part, passed the ordinary coast dwellers by.

Indeed, they remained rather a primitive lot and their lives went on as normal, hunting and foraging, their rude round huts still cold and smoky, their thatch roofs still leaking. The only noticeable difference was that now they had two masters to look to – the tribal leader and the Romans, with probably double taxes or tributes to pay.

Towards the end of the Roman occupation the Barbarians arrived. These new arrivals were predominantly Angles, Saxons and Jutes on a walkabout from northern Europe. They must have trodden lightly around the coastal settlements for there is little trace of their footsteps except in place names and thinly scattered archaeological reminders. For example, Bridlington was an Anglo-Saxon settlement whose name – Beohrtel's ton – meant 'the farm belonging to Beohrtel'; Mappleton, (Mapletree farm); Cleeton (Clay farm) and Hornsea Burton (fortified farm) all bear names of Anglo-Saxon origin which indicates some Anglo-Saxon presence.

In Hornsea the site of an Anglo-Saxon cemetery from the 6th century was uncovered during building works and about 18 burials complete with grave goods were discovered.

At Aldbrough there is some reason to believe that an older Saxon church once existed built by a gentleman by the name of Ulf – possibly the local bigwig before being displaced by William the Conqueror's mob.

Some authorities believe that it was the Saxons who gave Holderness its name. On finding the territory hollow between the cliffs of the coast and the Wolds, they named it Höll-deira-ness, hence the present Holderness.

Hot on the heels of the Barbarians came the Vikings. They too are credited with christening Holderness. This theory asserts that Holderness means the 'headland of the Hold'. A 'Hold' was a high-ranking man; 'ness' means headland.

Now if you had ever thought of mounting your own personal invasion of England then the Holderness coast is ideal, with many flat open beaches where an army can land with very little trouble. That is just what our Viking invaders did but whether they settled on the coast is a moot point. Viking place names do exist within the region but whether that indicates actual settlement is not certain.

At this time the coastline was cut into by a significant number of creeks and inlets. Many of these were navigable for the longships, putting the more desirable inland parts of East Yorkshire within reach. So, more than likely, these horned-helmeted warriors blinked once or twice and passed on by intent on investigating more profitable and less damp settlements… after all no-one wants to suffer rheumatism in their twilight years.

However, once they captured York in the late 9th century, the Viking invaders repented of their former looting and pillaging, disbanded and settled down to lives of relative domesticity. Then, their eyes may have turned back to the coast. It is possible that the village of Skipsea, now on the North Holderness coast but at that time much further inland, became a Viking administrative centre.

Large parts of the North of England, including Yorkshire, lived relatively quietly (give or take a feud or two) under Viking rule until the arrival of one William the Conqueror who thought he would take a tilt at the English throne. The Battle of Hastings on the south coast of England in 1066 changed everything.

Initially the Norman Conquest went largely unnoticed in Holderness – in fact most events of importance failed to register in this isolated part of the world until they were old hat elsewhere. After the Conquest however, rebellion smouldered and broke out intermittently in the North of England until eventually William became tired of it and, his patience at an end, killed off as many of the recalcitrant Northerners as he could, together with their families, pets and livestock. Not content with that early bout of ethnic cleansing he destroyed crops, salted the land to make it unfit for any further cultivation and made a wasteland of the North from the River Humber to the River Tees.

One of the other early actions our conquering hero took was the detailed survey of every town and village in England so he could understand better what exactly he had conquered and how much revenue he could raise through tax. This survey became the Domesday Book. The book was completed in 1086 and apart from showing how much of the north was by then just wasteland (just about all) it provides us with some detailed information about Holderness and its coastal settlements – some of which are now lost to the sea.

Today, reading through those details for this part of the world, I do wonder whether William regretted his harshness when he realised how much of the value of his northern lands he had wiped out – along with the people who worked them.

Once the natives had been subdued, Medieval society began to take shape. Broadly speaking it was made up of three elements – otherwise known as the Church, the Nobles and the Peasants. This division was supposed to work on the principle of everyone supporting everyone else – a churchman prayed for all, a knight or baron fought for all and a peasant worked for all – thus putting everyone firmly in their places.

Chapter Two

Footsteps on the Sands

This chapter introduces some of the lesser-known Holderness characters. Some were exports, taking their first breath on the coast before moving on to pastures new and some were imports from other places and countries. They were neither the richest nor the most intelligent, nor were they necessarily the eventual, major landowners of Holderness such as the Constables, Boyntons or Stricklands – their stories and achievements may be better found elsewhere. No, this identity parade offers a set of folk with their fair share of human weaknesses who, whether through design or happenchance, in their times, left a footstep on the sands of the Holderness coast.

THE RISE AND FALL OF DROGO DE LA BEUVRIERE

After his victory at the Battle of Hastings, William the Conqueror replaced the ruling Anglo-Saxon-Viking elite with Norman and French nobles and their supporters. Rebellion was ruthlessly crushed and the population held in check through a network of castles built across England.

Drogo de la Beuvriere became the Lord of Holderness' coastal communities living in one of these castles in Skipsea at the northern end of the coast. He was far from the *'parfit gentil knyght'* of Geoffrey Chaucer's *Canterbury Tales*. Drogo was in fact a Flemish mercenary with the conquering army and once the fighting and rebellion were all over he was very much in William's favour. As a token of his esteem William gave one of his nieces to Drogo in marriage.

With his title Earl of Holderness in the bag and marriage to one of William's nieces, Drogo's star would appear to be in the ascendant; opportunity was knocking but in one moment of madness he lost everything.

Drogo was, it seems, a man of uncertain temper; avaricious, barbaric on occasions and no-one, including his well-bred wife, was exempt from his explosive outbursts and brutish treatment. Whatever the reason, he went too far one day and murdered her (the gossips say by poison which he pretended was a love philtre) and buried her body somewhere in the castle. Perhaps he was a little slow on the uptake but it was not until he pondered on the corpse that he realised he could lose everything, including his head if he was found out.

At this point his mental faculties picked up speed; he saddled his fastest steed and rode hell for leather to William's court. There he bearded the great man himself and explained to William that he wanted to take his wife to meet her in-laws back in Flanders and could he please have permission for them to leave the country. William was clearly delighted by this idea of Drogo's domesticity and gave his permission. Whereupon, (as he was not one to lose hold of an opportunity), Drogo just happened to mention to William that although he was grateful for the fiefdom of Holderness it was poor country where few crops grew and, in short, Drogo's pockets were empty.

Fortified by a generous loan from uncle-in-law William, Drogo made haste over to the continent, took refuge in the Flemish court and was seen in this green and pleasant land no more – which is more than can be said for his wife. She apparently has been unable to find a resting place and for the past 900 years (according to folklore) has walked the lanes of Skipsea, sometimes headless, other times with head fully secured. Why, since she was poisoned, she should choose to haunt the good folk of Skipsea minus her head is something of a puzzle. Of late, however, no sightings have been recorded and we can only hope that she has found peace at last.

Major events of national importance never really appear to have disturbed the people of the Holderness coast who had fish to catch and farms to tend and enough chores to keep them busy until the Last Trump. However, one event – the signing of the Magna Carta by King John in 1215 closely affected one of our coastal landowners.

The Magna Carta was a first attempt to limit the powers of the King of England by a group of his most privileged subjects – the feudal barons – and formed the basis for the legal system. These barons were a wild bunch who owed duty and service to the king and in return they held huge tracts of land and ruled the roost over the locals. King John however, had a habit of whittling away at the rights and powers of the barons and matters came to a head in the early 13th century.

William II de Forz, Third Earl of Albermarle, Lord of Holderness and resident of Skipsea Castle was one of the 25 barons who acted as executors of the Magna Carta, and who was bit of a bad boy at that. He inherited vast estates from his mother, including most of Holderness.

Of all the executors of the Magna Carta, William was probably the one baron involved in this dust-up who directed less spite and venom towards the king, primarily because he was a man of remarkable flexibility of mind and principles.

When the people of London (an influential set at the time) came out to join forces with the other English barons in their opposition to the king, making the king's cause seem lost, our William took up with them.

After King John reneged on the charter and fighting between him and the barons broke out, William backed the king and returned to the royal cause.

When, in 1216 that cause once again appeared a lost and forlorn hope, so sweet William did turn his coat once again and re-join the winning side. He swung as it suited him, as though astride one of Newton's Cradles.

After King John died in 1216 William claimed to be new best friends with King Henry III but still he could not resist having a tantrum or two and fomenting a little local discontent. He was declared a rebel in 1219 and excommunicated. In 1220 he refused to surrender two of his castles so King Henry himself marched his army against them. Seeing their liege descending on them with some determination, the men of the garrisons took flight and the castles surrendered without a blow struck in anger. The king ordered the castle at Skipsea – headquarters of the Lord of Holderness- to be destroyed and eventually the land was leased for grazing.

Skipsea Castle today

The following year, we find William stirring up more trouble and he was excommunicated again but this time he had no castles in which to hide. He first sought sanctuary, then clemency and finally pardon – all of which were given provided he took himself off to the Holy Land for a six year sojourn to give everyone a rest from his tantrums. However, he was a stubborn fool and remained in England working with other turbulent spirits to stir up rebellion. It was not until one of his best buddies and co-conspirators, Falkes de Breauté fell from the king's grace, was excommunicated and permanently exiled that 'silly Billy' came to his senses and turned his coat one final time to stay loyal to Henry III. Whether the monarch regarded that as a 'Good Thing' is entirely a different matter.

LOCAL BOYS DONE GOOD

In the middle of the 14th century one of the most cataclysmic events occurred across England – the Black Death. This pestilence first arrived in the late spring or summer of 1348 and reached Yorkshire in 1349. It flourished in hot weather, and abated somewhat through the winter when it handed over its deadly duties to pneumonic plague. This form of plague spread through coughs and sneezes, allegedly giving rise to that chirpy child's rhyme *Ring o'Ring o'Roses*, 'A-tishoo, a-tishoo we all fall down'. Estimates from those in the know suggest that within three years a third to a half of Britain's population was wiped out. Whole communities died and villages were abandoned.

Manpower was suddenly scarce and hence more valuable. The peasants could negotiate better terms for their labour, marking the beginnings of a change from tied labourers to wage earners. More land became available to those who survived and gave rise to a new set of relatively wealthy small landowners and yeomen farmers. The working population found it easier to move around – either to areas where workers had been wiped out or to the developing towns.

Despite the efforts of the king and nobles to crush these green shoots of independence the feudal system all across England began to crumble and change was in the air. Ordinary folk started to wake up and question why they needed the fellow in the big house up the top end of the village to lord it over them. This is a period that marks the rise of the merchant class – the self-made men who eventually formed the middle class.

Fine specimens of this new class in society were the De la Pole brothers William and Richard, successful wool merchants who, before moving to Hull, hailed from Ravenser, one of the medieval Holderness coastal towns that now lies under the North Sea. They arrived at their wealth through wool export but the brothers swelled the family coffers by lending huge wads of cash to their royal highnesses Edward II and Edward III.

Richard began to spend more of his time carrying out various duties and services for the king which took him overseas leaving younger brother William to manage the merchant business. When Richard went to live in London in 1331 they dissolved their 20-year partnership. The document recording this is a model of brotherly love as they each *'forgave all manner of injuries done, said and thought from the time of coming into the world to the writing of this deed'*, as well as freeing each other from any joint obligations. Then they divvied up the spoils of the business which were not inconsiderable.

William continued to serve as the king's personal credit card. He became the first mayor of Hull and fitted out ships with men and munitions for the king's futile wars against the Scots. In 1339 he redeemed, almost certainly with his own money, part of the crown jewels which the king had pawned for 50,000 gold florins. The king, whose debt to him by this time exceeded £100,000 in old money, created him the Chief Baron of the Exchequer and that caused a snag.

Edward III was not a miserly king; he liked to live well, go to war now and then to keep his people on their toes and had no problem with living way beyond his means. To fund another minor war in France he demanded money not of William but of the kingdom. He wanted tithes, taxes and a vast number of sacks of wool to sell. William, who had readily mortgaged all he owned, would not mortgage the country. He told the king that the amount he demanded could not be raised without the very great likelihood of his having a war with his own people, never mind the French.

Edward was majorly miffed, threw his loyal and honest banker in jail and withdrew all the privileges and possessions he had given him. A charge of wool smuggling (probably trumped up) was levied against him. To obtain a pardon the wily old royal made William wipe out all the royal debts, as well as give up his estates in Burstwick near Hull. Nevertheless, there was still plenty left for William to undertake a series of charitable works back in Hull before he died in 1366.

Peg Fyfe – An Enemy for Life

Not all of the footprints left behind on the Holderness coast belong to nobles and notables. The coastal villages had their fair share of saints and sinners amongst the ordinary people and in the 17th century Peg Fyfe was most certainly not a woman to cross.

The little village of Kilnsea squats right down on the southern tip of the Holderness coast, open to all the elements and particularly the depredations of the sea. It was the setting for a terrible, gory crime committed by Peg Fyfe. Some claimed she was a witch, some doubted it. But what everyone was certain of was that she led a band of ruffians who practised theft and extortion with equal aplomb.

Peg had her eye on some horses belonging to a Kilnsea farmer. One day she cornered the farmer's servant lad and threatened him with the direst consequences to terrify him into leaving the stable door open one night so she could perpetrate the theft. She promised that should he reveal the plot to anyone she would skin him alive.

The lad, being of stout Yorkshire stock and therefore having more wits about him than most, was, nonetheless, torn between his terror of Peg and his sense of loyalty to his gaffer. He tossed and turned on his straw mattress trying to work out what to do.

On the day of the intended theft, the lad had his bright idea. In the morning he asked the farmer to come to the stable and look at one of the horses. There, in front of his gaffer, he whispered to the horses telling them that Peg Fyfe was coming to steal them that very night – thus neatly letting the farmer know what game was afoot whilst not spilling the beans directly. How the lad thought that this niceness of integrity would save him should Peg get to hear of it I cannot tell; perhaps after all his wits had gone a-wandering.

That night, when Peg and her mob came to steal the horses they found themselves on the receiving end of a load of lead shot but despite being injured she and the gang got clean away.

For weeks after the attack the boy laid low, terrified of going anywhere for fear of Peg. He never strayed from the farmyard. But as weeks turned to months and nothing more was heard of the gang, the lad forgot his fears and started to roam further and further afield until one day whilst wandering far from the farm, members of the robber gang recognised him and snatched him up. The gang took the boy to Peg who, unappreciative of the subtleties of the lad's strategy, ignored his pleading that he had only told the horses about the plot and made good her promise to flay the poor boy alive. It is said (by whom is unrecorded!) that despite his agony as the skin was stripped he uttered no sound until Peg started on the skin on his palms and soles of his feet. At that moment he emitted a terrible, piteous cry, heard far out at sea.

When she finished with him, somehow the lad managed to crawl home, a bloody mass, before giving up his last on his doorstep. The charming Peg and some of her gang were later captured and hanged for their many crimes.

AN ORDINARY MAN OF PRINCIPLE

The 17th century saw the rise of non-conformism across England and one of the earliest sects was the Society of Friends – the Quakers. A visit by George Fox to Holderness in 1651 kindled interest in the beliefs and principles of the Friends. Up and down the coast a small tireless group took The Word to villages and hamlets and one man, a fisherman from Kilnsea by the name of Richard Sellars heard The Word.

At the time Britain was at war with the Dutch and the British Navy was always on the lookout for new recruits. One way of obtaining these recruits was through the pressgang – an ugly form of conscription that allowed gangs to take law-abiding citizens in ports and coastal villages and whisk them away to serve, willy-nilly in the Royal Navy ships.

In 1665, whilst in Scarborough (then a fishing village on the North Yorkshire coast) the pressgang caught Richard. He refused to go on board the ketch that was collecting up these new crews and was badly beaten before being hoisted onto the ship with a tackle. The ketch worked on behalf of the Ship of the Line (a powerful warship that was lined up with other ships to pound the enemy with cannon), the *Royal Prince* and it took Richard and the other pressganged men first to Bridlington and then onwards to the Nore – a sandbank at the mouth of the River Thames and an assembly point for the navy. At the Nore, Richard was hauled aboard the *Royal Prince* and the following day was ordered to work at the capstan. This he refused to do and to compound the situation he also refused to eat. Quakers were, and are, pacifists and to fight or assist warfare was completely against their beliefs. His stance was a brave one given the harsh conditions under which the men of the king's navy worked.

1780 caricature of a pressgang

Richard received a flogging from the boatswain and then the captain sent for him, demanding to know why he would not fight for the king and why he would not eat. Richard's reply was a gentle one, *'I told him I was afraid to offend God, therefore I could not fight with carnal weapons.'* The captain replied to this piety with yet another flogging before one of the crew begged for mercy on Richard's behalf. *'I pray you, noble captain, be merciful, for I know him to be an honest man.'* To which the captain is alleged to have replied, *'He is a Quaker and I will beat his brains out'*.

According to Richard's account, three days later Admiral Sir Edward Spragge came aboard the *Royal Prince* and learned that a Quaker had been pressed aboard his ship. He learned too that the boatswain's mate had refused to flog Richard anymore and so demoted him and took his cane – a mark of his position on board – from him. The disgrace was taken in good part and with some relief by the mate who had been affected by Richard's principled stance and quiet yet determined demeanour.

The – shall we say – unusual behaviour from some of his crew members caused the admiral some concern. This fiery Irishman himself was no stranger to controversy. He held to the king during the English Civil War yet fought for the Dutch during the first Anglo-Dutch war; he became a pirate and married a pirate's daughter before being returned to grace when Charles II was restored to the English throne. He was always popular with his sailors. Yet Richard's apparently pervasive, gentle influence on members of the *Royal Prince's* crew caused the admiral to take a hard line. He called the whole ship's company together and, in front of them clapped Richard in irons. He then addressed the crew, saying:

'Gentlemen, sailors, and soldiers, and whosoever sails under me for the king, on board his Majesty's ship the Royal Prince... take notice there is a man called a Quaker, who is to be laid in irons during the king's pleasure and mine, for refusing to fight and to eat of the king's victuals; therefore I charge you all and every man, that none of you sell or give him any victuals, meat, drink, or water, for if you do, you shall have the same punishment.'

Despite this warning some members of the crew treated Richard kindly, particularly the carpenter's mate who surreptitiously tried to share his rations with him. However there were other prisoners with Richard who continued to abuse him to such an extent that one of the younger officers went to the admiral to try and put an end to the ill use. The admiral had Richard taken out of irons and called a council of war with the captains of his fleet to decide what to do about Richard. As a compromise, they offered him a place on a small ship that acted as a tender; however it also carried guns. True to his principles, Richard declined this way out and said he would stay on board the *Royal Prince* and see out his punishment. With no other alternative, the admiral then sentenced Richard to death.

When this was generally known at least two of the crew begged for Richard's life. Again this was a brave act on their part – to plead for a convicted criminal's life to their admiral risked their own lives as well.

The following day at eight o'clock, with the noose hanging from the yardarm, Richard came forward to meet his fate and, ultimately, his Maker. But as he stepped onto the gunwale, Admiral Spragge called for silence. In an extraordinary twist of events, he proclaimed Richard a free man, *'as free as any on board the ship'*. Why he did this is not clear. Did his conscience stir him? Was he concerned about the effect on his crew that the hanging of a pious man who had done nothing more than hold to his beliefs would have? Whatever his reason, he had cause later to be thankful that he gave Richard his life back and that, in an unexplained compromise, Richard agreed to act as a non-combatant on the ship. As a non-combatant Richard's duty was to carry down the wounded and to look out for fire ships.

A few days later the *Royal Prince* engaged with the Dutch fleet and Richard, seeing the ship heading towards some shoals and in danger of being stranded and overhauled by the Dutch, called out a warning to the pilot. Just in time, the pilot steered the ship into deeper water and safety. As the battle continued, Richard then spied a fire ship bearing down on their starboard bow and again his timely warning averted disaster. After the battle, his actions drew the attention of the admiral who remarked, *'It would have been a great pity had his life been taken before the engagement'*.

A week later after another engagement with the Dutch, the ship sailed for England. The admiral called Richard to him, gave him his freedom and instructed the captain of the *Royal Prince* to write out a certificate to that effect. And there, we leave the quiet fisherman to disappear into the mists of time.

ADAM ALVIN – THE MURDEROUS MANSERVANT

Whether Adam Alvin thought on the lines *'all for love and the world well lost'* or whether he had a more mercenary motive we shall never know. What we can surmise is that the man must have had a devilish charm and a persuasive tongue about him... what else could make apparently well-bred, well-brought up young women throw caution to the wind and cast their lot with him? You be the judge.

In 1708 Adam Alvin was a man intending to rise in the world – an opportunist with an eye for a fortune. He worked as manservant to the Reverend Enoch Sinclair, the vicar of Owthorne, then a village towards the southern end of the Holderness coast.

Adam had his eye upon Mary Sinclair the elder niece (and heiress) of Rev Sinclair. Eventually, he declared his love for her and she vowed that she returned his affections. At this point, realising that his employer was unlikely to view a relationship between them with any approbation and would therefore prove an obstacle to the couple's happiness, Adam decided that 'Something Must Be Done'. The something was murder – carried out with the full knowledge, not to say connivance of both Mary and her younger sister who also shared Sinclair's household.

The deed done, the three of them put it about the neighbourhood that the Rev Sinclair had gone visiting on horseback. On investigation later, his horse was found, fully tacked up but without its rider. Despite an extensive search no trace of the reverend was found. The marriage of Adam and Mary took place soon after these events.

However, the reverend's parishioners were a suspicious lot and the gossip started. Adam, Mary and her younger sister all fled to London to escape it. There they lived for four years – all that time waiting for a loud knock on the door at midnight.

When the younger sister was taken mortally ill, she confessed about the murder and revealed where they had hidden Rev Sinclair's body. The knock on the door finally came.

The body was recovered from a ditch near the house, and Adam and Mary arrested and tried in York. Mary was acquitted but Adam was sentenced to hang. During the preaching of the condemned sermon – a practice designed to send the guilty off in a proper frame of mind – Adam loudly declared his innocence. Scarcely had the words left his mouth when the preacher, a Mr Mace, dropped down stone dead. Not one to miss an opportunity, Adam shouted out that the hand of God had shown itself in support of his innocence and he almost convinced the congregation that it was so. However, sanity returned the following day and Adam was hanged, confessing his crime at the very last.

The church, the vicarage and the village of Owthorne where the dastardly deed was done have long given themselves up to the sea and now the murder of the Reverend Enoch Sinclair is merely a footnote in time.

Chapter Three

Humble Habits

Most of England had converted to Christianity by the 7th century and this led to a boom time for building churches, cathedrals and monasteries. English monasteries were at the heart of the church, often sponsored by local rulers. During the Viking raids of the 9th century these communities were a target for looting and pillaging but also suffered from take-overs by an acquisitive, not to say greedy, nobility. The end result was that by the beginning of the 10th century, there were few useful religious communities, monastic lands and finances were not in a healthy state and the quality of any religious work done was often quite poor.

After the Norman Conquest, William replaced most of the existing religious leaders with a new and powerful set of Norman and French churchmen. This placed the church in the premier league as far as power goes, with the men of the cloth taking precedence in society and growing in wealth and influence – all provided they supported the feudal system and king. Monasteries back in Normandy received grants of English lands which allowed them to branch out and build daughter priories and monastic cells in what seemed to them an almost heathen kingdom.

Along our Holderness coast the Bishop of Durham and the Archbishop of York both held large estates as did the Abbeys of Meaux, near Beverley, St Mary's in Bridlington and Thornton in Lincolnshire, as well as the Priories of Swine and Nunkeeling. These communities exerted considerable influence over the lives of those living at the coast and so from time to time we will dip into their stories too.

The Founding of Meaux Abbey

The story of the founding of Meaux Abbey has much to do with the age and girth of one William le Gros, Count of Aumale who was at the time (around 1151) the Lord of Holderness. Now, Fat Willy had a problem. In his younger and slimmer days he had taken a vow to make a pilgrimage to the Holy Land. However this was one of those things in life that just kept getting put off until in 1150, elderly and with a waistline that you would need a week to walk around, Willy looked for a way to be released from his vow.

A chance meeting with Adam, a monk from Fountains Abbey with a talent for architecture, provided the solution. Willy could be released from his promise to pilgrimage if he stumped up the funds to establish a religious community. Adam selected what he considered a suitable site, thumping his staff on the ground to proclaim his choice. Unfortunately, Willy had already earmarked the land for his own hunting playground (although with his girth, it is a puzzle as to what beast could possibly have carried him during the hunt) and tried to convince Adam that other, more worthy sites were available. But Adam was nothing if not determined. He stood firm and the abbey was built in 1151, populated by monks from Fountains Abbey and led by Adam who presided as abbot until 1160.

Perhaps, after all, Fat Willy had the last belly laugh. The site Adam chose was not the best. It was located about 12 miles inland from the coast, in the flood plain of the River Hull. Although amply provided with water, woodland and pasture, the land around was marshy and liable to flood, causing the abbey severe problems at times. In fact, the community at Meaux was regularly beset with difficulties. When the plague struck in the mid-13th century only ten out of the 50 monks survived; the abbey struggled almost continuously against debt; it suffered lawsuits and conflict both internally and with other religious communities.

However for an historian, the chronicles of Meaux Abbey written by one of the abbots provide a rich insight not only into the life and times of the abbey but also of events happening in the wider world of medieval England. The chronicles contain fascinating snippets such as the *'discovery of King Arthur's body at Glastonbury'* or news of a thick fog that descended in London whilst the Bishop of London was officiating in St. Paul's. Thunder and lightning and a *'most foul stench'* accompanied the fog so that the congregation deserted the cathedral leaving only the bishop there with one attendant.

And there we too will leave the Meaux monks, although we shall meet them again from time to time in this short history.

THE NAUGHTY NUNS OF NUN KEELING

Squabbles and disagreements were not just the prerogative of monks. The Benedictine nunnery at Nunkeeling, an inland Holderness village which owned land and property along the coast seemed to be moved by the spirit of disobedience and rebellion every now and again.

The nunnery came into being in 1152 with a prioress and 12 nuns. All seemed to be going well enough there for the first century or so, apart from the fact that the nuns were so poor they did not have enough money to feed and clothe themselves. That problem appears to have been overcome and it was not until 1314 that we learn of intransigence and naughty habits.

To smother this licentious behaviour, the Archbishop of York issued a number of rules:

1 No nun to miss services because she is engrossed in her sewing or other more absorbing tasks.
2 All doors to be locked and diligently checked to be so; all keys to be held by the sub-prioress and one other worthy woman.

24

3 The sub-prioress to investigate who had been stealing the alms given to the nunnery and if it was the *elemosinaria* (the nun whose task it was to distribute alms) or if it were proved she was negligent she must be removed from office.

4 No young nun *'concerning whom sinister suspicion might arise'* may consort with or have meals with the lay brothers nor with any other man, inside or outside the nunnery, except she be chaperoned by an older nun.

(There is no further explanation of *'sinister suspicion'* but I guess that the old archbishop was concerned that girls will be girls.)

5 No nun to look dashing by wearing designer accessories of the day such as a flashy girdle, high-heeled shoes or anything else in the clothing line unsuitable for a religious house.

6 No nun to be allowed out except on nunnery business or to visit friends and relatives, in which case she must be accompanied by a worthy nun.

The same year as the archbishop issued his rules one of the nuns, Isabella St Quintin, held the post of cellarer which was an important role within the community. However, in front of all the other nuns (big disgrace), he ordered her to be removed from this office; forbade her to hold any further office and ordered her to keep within the nunnery walls. Clearly she had offended his sensibilities in some way although he is too coy to reveal the full story.

For some time afterwards, it did seem that the ladies of the nunnery obeyed the rules but their rebellious fires were merely damped down rather than extinguished.

Isabella appears to have remained popular with the other nuns because a couple of years after the archbishop's rules, they all voted her the new prioress. The Men of the See of York (dean and chapter on this occasion) were having none of this and quashed the election, claiming a breach of canonical procedure. However, their choice, Avice de la More, did no better and in 1318 they found themselves having to order her to desist from her *'conspiracies, rebellions and disobedience'* on pain of losing her retirement pension. Presumably she had regulated the nuns in a rather lax way as other examples of non-nunlike behaviour come to light.

Dionisia Dareyns was to be incarcerated in the nunnery on account of her disobedience and to be disciplined every Friday. Avice de Lelle was most strictly forbidden to have any dealings with Robert de Eton, the chaplain and she too was locked up after she confessed her *'incontinence'* with him and ordered to do penance.

The following year, the poor archbishop was forced to enquire yet again into the *'rebellious nuns of the house of Keeling'* since information had reached his chaste ears that some of the ladies of that nunnery had ignored their vows of obedience and devotion and engaged in intrigues. They had revealed secrets of the chapter to secular persons. On top of all that, he learned *'with a bitter heart'* that our Avice had yet again broken her vows of obedience and submission to the prioress. Such was life in the nunnery of Nunkeeling – one of our coastal landowners.

The ruins of Nunkeeling Priory Chapel

ONE OF THE RICHEST

Bridlington Priory was founded around 1113 by Walter de Gant. Over its lifetime kings and nobles favoured the priory and gifted lands and churches, not only from along the Holderness coast but across Yorkshire too, in the hope of saving their bacon in the afterlife.

Perhaps the habit was catching (no pun intended) but just as the Nunkeeling nuns needed a watchful eye keeping on them so the Bridlington brothers appeared to commit certain transgressions requiring the intervention of the Archbishop of York.

Archbishop Wickwane issued several injunctions to the Bridlington brothers. In particular:

1 No brother to dodge services by feigning illness.
2 The prior to listen to the wisdom of the elders and not to the younger members of the community.

3 No sporting dogs or horses to be kept.

4 No ladies allowed within the monastery precincts excepting where it would inconvenience great ladies to be kept waiting outside.

5 Drinking after compline is strictly forbidden.

6 Buffoons who raise laughter are to be repelled.

However, in 1363 the priory elected its most notable prior – John de Thwing – a man of genuine piety and goodness who ruled the priory with conscientious care for 17 years. Shortly after his death stories emerged of the miracles he had performed and eventually a commission reported to the pope concerning John's miracles. These included walking on the sea to rescue men in a rowing boat, bringing five people back to life and the old water into wine trick. Pope Boniface IX canonised him, creating St John of Bridlington and his body was placed in a shrine behind the high altar which became a place of pilgrimage. October 10th became his Feast Day and the pope decreed that all penitents who on that day visited the tomb would be granted relaxation of the normal period of penance. No doubt that drew the crowds.

GEORGE RIPLEY AND THE SECRET OF THE PHILOSOPHER'S STONE

We cannot leave Bridlington Priory without a brief mention of George Ripley who was a canon there. George worked something of a portfolio career in the heady years of the 15th century. He pursued not only his religious vocation, but also became an 'expert' alchemist, chamberlain to the pope and financial backer (allegedly) of the Knights of St John of Jerusalem in Rhodes when they were hassled by the Turks. In between times, he fitted in a marriage (permissible in those days for churchmen) and sired two sons.

George left the priory, where he had studied the Physical Sciences, and travelled to Europe, living for a while in Rome where Pope Innocent VIII took a shine to him and created him Chamberlain and Master of Ceremonies. In 1478 he returned to these shores and, wrapped in his bony bosom, (OK, poetic licence here – we don't know what he looked like) lay 'The Secret' – that of Transmutation.

He revealed this secret in his best known alchemical opus, *The Compound of Alchemy* – something like a 16th century *Alchemy for Dummies* – in which he discloses *'the right and perfectest meanes'* to make the Philosopher's Stone – that elusive stuff that magicks rusty old scrap metal into gold and silver and, as an added bonus, produces the 'I want to live forever' juice, also known as The Elixir of Life. This work, written in verse, describes the 12 stages or 'gates' of the alchemical process. A century later his recipe was translated into pictures in the Ripley Scrolls.

Ripley shuffled off his own mortal coil around 1490 and achieved post-mortem stardom when *The Compound of Alchemy* became a best seller. That and his other works contributed to a resurgence of interest in alchemy, particularly in the following couple of centuries. Here is the first verse from the first of the 12 gates.

CALCINATION – THE FIRST GATE
Calcination is the purgation of our stone,
And restoration also of its natural heat.
Of radical humidity it looseth none,
Inducing solution into our stone most mete.
Seek after philosophy I you advise
But not after the common guise,
With sulphur and salts prepared in diverse ways.

Sometimes the squabbles and disagreements between the abbeys gave their workers cause to stand, stare and wonder at the antics of their Betters. Take for example the brangle over boundaries and fishing at Hornsea Mere between Meaux Abbey and St Mary's Abbey, York.

Hornsea Mere

In the 13th century, both these abbeys held fishing rights on Hornsea Mere – a large lake teeming with toothsome fish located on the outskirts of Hornsea town. Each community had its own area of the mere within which it could take fish but the boundary between the two areas was in dispute. Unable to resolve their disagreement through prayer and persuasion, the abbots of each community opted for trial by combat.

Trial by combat or *Duellum* was a method of resolving disputes imported to England by the all-conquering Normans. Each party to the dispute hired champions to fight on their behalf and last man standing was the winner. Once the champions agreed to battle on behalf of their paymaster, they gave the judge in the dispute a gauntlet with one penny in each of the fingers. Coming to the arena suitably dressed for the rumble, each champion swore an oath affirming the rightness of their paymaster's cause. They also solemnly promised they were not concealing charms or other magic talismans and had eschewed all forms of sorcery. It was to be a fair fight.

Now the Abbot of Meaux at the time was probably a bit more worldly than his adversary and he mopped up the market for champions by employing seven of the best around at great cost to the abbey. In monopolising the market in this way he forced St Mary's to employ the left-overs and, by inference, the less accomplished.

The appointed day of battle dawned, the disputed boundary marked out and the champions set to, no doubt watched by a host of bemused locals and noisy supporters.

Trial by combat only ended when one party was dead or cried 'Craven!' to submit. The abbots' champions knocked seven bells out of each other for most of the day before – shock, horror – the men of Meaux submitted and owned themselves beat.

Imagine the chagrin of the Abbot of Meaux after going to all that effort to secure the best and especially when back in his treasure house he counted the cost of his failed endeavour.

THE DISSOLUTION OF THE MONASTERIES

One of the principal actions of King Henry VIII (apart from a regular change of wife) was the Dissolution of the Monasteries – legal measures that disbanded monasteries, priories, friaries and convents. Through this process, Henry took to his ample bosom the wealth previously enjoyed by these communities; he disposed of their assets and, when he remembered, provided for the inmates.

At first only communities with an income of less than £200 per year were affected. Any valuable metals they possessed were taken to be melted down and added to the king's coffers. Henry rented out their lands and other possessions not required by him or his government were sold off. The local population was swift to dismantle and recycle building stone, bricks, timber and anything else that might prove useful.

The recalcitrant folk of the North of England disagreed with Henry's fundraising policy and a movement called the Pilgrimage of Grace arose in 1536. A gathering of 9,000 men led by Robert Aske marched on York with the intention of restoring the monks to their monastery. This movement was supported by many of the northern nobles, including several who held the lives and livelihoods of our coastal dwellers in their hands. These included the Lord of Holderness himself, Lord Darcy, as well as three from branches of the East Yorkshire Constable family – Sirs William, Robert and John.

Eventually Henry issued promises and pardons to the leaders of the Pilgrimage; promises to accede to some requests and pardons for those who took part. However, a later rebellion by these stiff-necked northerners, probably caused by Henry's reneging on his promises, meant that Darcy and all three of the Constables were executed. Sir Robert's death being supervised by the Duke of Norfolk, who informed his king that:

'On Frydaye, beyng market daye at Hull, Sir Robert Constable suffred, and dothe hang above the highest gate of the towne, so trymmed in cheynes, that I thinke his bones will hang there this hundrethe yere.'

Clearly there was nothing like a good hanging to while away the time in between doing the weekly shop on market day.

However, this was not enough for our Henry. He needed more funds and having grabbed the goodies from the smaller communities, turned a covetous eye towards the larger ones including the landowners along the Holderness coast – Bridlington Priory, Meaux Abbey and Nunkeeling Priory.

Meaux Abbey was surrendered on December 11th 1539 by Richard Stopes, the last abbot. The buildings were demolished and the stones used for building defences around the town of Hull. The remaining members of the abbey were pensioned off – the abbot received a pension of £40 per year, the prior one of £6 and the monks received between £5 and £6 each. At the dissolution the gross value of the abbey and its assets was just under £450. Most of the abbey lands were given to the Earl of Warwick, a big pal of Henry's.

Nunkeeling Priory was surrendered rather later in 1540 when 12 nuns were housed there, together with about 25 other people who lived or worked there. Its goodies went to Richard Gresham, a wealthy textile merchant who kept Henry in velvets and satins but the priory remained as the parish church until it fell into disrepair.

Bridlington Priory provided rich pickings for Henry as it was one of the wealthiest in Yorkshire with an annual income just shy of £550 (over £170,000 in today's money) from lands stretching all the way down the Holderness coast to Spurn Point and much further inland. In 1537 the last prior William Wode wrote to Thomas Cromwell, the king's henchman in the dissolution business, pleading for the abbey to be spared. It was not. The abbey was demolished in 1539, apart from two buildings, one of which became the parish church for the town and the other, the Bayle Gate which, (after a varied career), is now a museum. Prior Wode himself took part in the Pilgrimage of Grace and was later executed for his pains. Stone from the priory was taken away and used to build quays in the town.

We can get a good idea of what would have happened to the Bridlington buildings from a letter written to Thomas Cromwell by Richard Bellycys, one of the monastic demolition men. In it he writes of the destruction of a similar abbey, Jervaulx Abbey in North Yorkshire. He tells Cromwell that he stripped the lead off the roof but it cannot be sent until the next summer because of the state of the roads:

'Pleasythe your good Lordshipp to be advertysed. I have taken downe all the lead of Jervayse, and made itt in pecys of half-foders, which lead amounteth to the numbre of eighteen score and five foders, with thirty and foure foders, and a half, that were there before. And they said lead cannot be conveit, nor caryed unto the next sombre, for the ways in that contre are so foule, and deep, that no carrage, can passe in wyntre.'

He continues by asking for guidance as to what to do with the bells:

'... And as concerning the selling of the bells I cannot sell them above 15s. the hundreth, wherein I would gladly know your Lordshipps pleasor, whether I should sell them after that price, or send them up to London. And if they be sent up surely the carriage wol be costly frome that place to the water.'

He then goes on to suggest that because winter is drawing in he should leave Bridlington Priory until the following summer although he is anxious to assure Cromwell that he will do the job with the utmost efficiency:

'And as for Byrdlington I have doyn nothing there as yet, but sparethe itt to March next, bycause the days now are so short,

34

and from such tyme as I begyn I trust shortly to dyspatche it after such fashion that when all is fynished, I trust your Lordshipp shall that think that I have bene no evyll howsbound in all such things, as your Lordshipp haith appoynted me to do.'

In all, Henry gathered land and rents from some 616 abbeys across England, worth about £20 million in today's money. His people held a forlorn hope that there would be no more need for taxes and that some of the money would be used to found schools. True, Henry strengthened his navy with some of the cash and a few new bishoprics were founded, but most of the wealth went into his coffers and those of his court. No abbot sat in the House of Lords, and for the first time the nobles had a majority in that house. These nobles and landlords grew fat on the property of the monasteries and took care to see that what King Henry had done would never be undone.

The Bayle Gate, Bridlington Priory

Chapter Four
Give Us Our Daily Bread

In the very early days Holderness Coastal Man kept body and soul together by fishing, fowling, hunting and a bit of farming. Many of the earliest settlements along the coastline were located near mere sites. Eels were taken from Skipsea Mere and fish from Hornsea Mere. The area was on bird migration routes and provided breeding grounds for waterfowl.

However, the watery and damp nature of Holderness meant that from Roman times onwards landowners, and particularly the monasteries and nobles, made various attempts to improve the drainage of the area so that they could increase output and hence tithes and taxes. In addition, the nobles needed their land farming and their castles cleaned; the monasteries needed lay people to see to their menial tasks, and all in all a job market began to develop.

THE MEDIEVAL JOB MARKET

The manor and its lord were the foundation stones of Medieval society and provided employment for the peasants in the form of tied labour… the days of a man (or woman) being worthy of their hire had not quite arrived. Theoretically the health, wealth and happiness of both the lord and his minions, the peasants, were tied in together.

Many of the manors on the Holderness coast were held by the Lords of Holderness who, in turn, granted them to other lesser nobles, called vassals, in exchange for military service. Vassals might also sublet further. So, for example, at Aldbrough, halfway down the coast, Drogo (before his disgrace) was Lord of Holderness; the manor was held by William de Ros on his behalf and he, in turn sublet lands to John of Beverley and his son. Some manors were held directly by the king and in some cases, the lordship was given away to be held by the church or a monastery.

Acting as the middle man between Lord of the Manor and his great unwashed was the reeve. He was a manor official appointed by the lord or elected by the peasants and dealt with day-to-day issues such as organising the work in the lord's fields.

The peasant class had its own hierarchy. First came the serfs and the villeins (not to be confused with the 'hiss-boo' type of villain although this probably did apply in some cases). These were classes of peasants who paid the lord certain dues in return for land that they could farm for themselves. The dues were usually in the form of labour on the lord's land sometimes up to three days in a week. They were tied to the manor where they lived and could not move away without the lord's permission and that of the Lord of the Manor where they intended to move. Basically, they were regarded as part of the goods and chattels belonging to the manor and sold with it into the service of whoever bought the land.

Moving on down the food chain we come to the cottager – a low status peasant with a cottage but with little or no land who generally worked as a simple labourer; and the servants who worked in the lord's manor house, doing the cooking, cleaning, laundering and other household chores.

In addition there were smaller landowners, often called yeoman farmers. Yet even they could not escape duties on behalf of the Lord of the Manor. At the least, they had to have arms (as in weapons) and train with a bow ready to do service to protect the nobility.

Apart from earning a daily crust tending livestock and working in the fields, medieval peasants could find opportunities for work in fisheries, hunting, netting or otherwise trapping wildfowl such as duck, geese and swan or trapping eels. The larger settlements, particularly where there was a castle, such as the one at Skipsea, offered a wider choice of career – as a blacksmith, baker, candle-maker, carpenter or brewer, for example.

As the area was deforested and timber became scarce peat became an important source of fuel along with whin or furze. Peasants could work at peat cutting on behalf of the abbeys or Lord of the Manor. Additionally, 'turbary' – the right to cut and take away peat – was an important right in terms of providing fuel for their own winter hearths. The carrs and wetlands created ideal cutting grounds and many settlements along the coast such as Barmston, Skipsea, Cleeton (now under the sea) and Tunstall had their own sites for cutting.

The later Middle Ages saw men shake off the shackles of serfdom and begin to strike out on their own. Settlements like Bridlington and Hornsea grew into small towns with regular markets and fairs and folk trading on their own behalf. With such development came new careers, trading opportunities and the possibility to move to one of the medieval new towns inland such as Beverley or Hull where work could be found.

One constant for the Holderness coastal dwellers in all the hubble-bubble of changing times was the life-sustaining, life-taking North Sea and there would be something fishy about a chapter concerned with making a living on the coast where there was no mention of fishing.

FISHING IN THE BLOOD

As we have seen from earliest times of settlement along the coast fishing formed a way of earning the daily bread. For some it was done to feed family and friends; for others it was a trading livelihood.

Bridlington, Hornsea and Hornsea Beck (until it disappeared under the sea) had fishing fleets and quays for landing the catch. However, the place that epitomised fishing as a livelihood (and which still does to some extent) was the village of Flamborough, the northernmost outpost of the Holderness coast.

The village has two coves, known as North and South Landings and from the beaches of these coves the muscular men (and women) of Flamborough launched their fishing cobles and landed their catches. At one time it was impossible to walk through the little village without tripping over a fisherman – fishing was in the genes; sons followed fathers who had followed their fathers to fish and to trap crabs and lobster. In 1794 a storm at sea took the lives of 20 fishermen and nearly every house in Flamborough mourned the loss of a family member.

After author and hiker Walter White visited Flamborough he described the sights in his book, *A Month in Yorkshire,* written in the mid 19th century:

'Here I saw some 60 or 80 boats, perched from top to bottom of the steep slope; and groups of fishermen with their families, men, women and children all busy with preparations for the herring fishery... ' and adds rather obviously, *'while about there prevailed a strong fishy smell.'*

The boats used by the fishermen were a throwback to Viking days. Known as cobles, their shallow keels made them very stable and suitable for launching and recovering from a beach. They were initially powered by sail and oars, and were hauled on and off the beach using manpower or horsepower. When the mechanical age caught up, engines and tractors became the power source of preference. Indeed Flamborough and other beach-launching sites were places where old tractors went to die. The sea water corroded their innards so it was not worth having a brand-new shiny model.

The fishermen were early risers and went out around 4 or 5 am to a distance of up to 10 miles and returned with their catches five or six hours later. Once the catch was landed the men and their families packed it into baskets, creels and boxes and hauled it by donkey, mule or manpowered sledge up the steep slipway to the village. There carts and then, in time, wagons waited to move the catch on to towns and cities inland.

Flamborough North Landing

A HEAD FOR HEIGHTS

In summer, to supplement their income, Flamborough fishermen would take out shooting parties so that intrepid sportsmen could take random pot-shots at the seabirds nesting and roosting on the high chalk cliffs of Flamborough. Naturalist and all-round Yorkshire eccentric, Charles Waterton wrote:

'He… will feel sad at heart on learning the unmerited persecution to which these harmless seafowl are exposed. Parties of sportsmen from all quarters of the kingdom visit Flamborough and its vicinity during the summer months and

spread sad devastation around them. No profit attends the carnage, the poor unfortunate birds merely serve as marks to aim at and they are generally left where they fall.'

However, revolted as he was by the indiscriminate slaughter, Waterton nevertheless wanted to take a closer look at the habits of seabirds in the area around Flamborough and (as was his wont) chose to get as close as possible to the nests. The notion of descending the cliffs in a rope sling held no terrors for the man who had wrestled a crocodile in South America and climbed up the roof of St Peter's in Rome to leave his gloves on the lightening conductor.

His desire to see the seabirds at close quarters introduced him to the 'climmers' or egg-gathers – another way the fishermen and farmers of Flamborough found to supplement their incomes – all provided they had a good head for heights and partners in whom they could place implicit trust.

Climming was usually a family occupation with different families having their 'own' bit of coast to work on. A team of between two and four men worked together with one being lowered over the cliff and steadied by the others. It was dangerous work for the man over the cliff, wearing only a cloth cap stuffed with straw, his hands wrapped with dried grass or straw to stop the rope from cutting them. This was Waterton's description in 1834:

'... he who is to descend now puts his legs through a pair of hempen braces which meet around his middle and there form a waistband. A man now holds the rope firmly in his hand and gradually lowers his comrade down the precipice. While he is descending... he passes from ledge to ledge and rock to rock. It requires considerable address on the part of the descending climber to save himself from being hit by fragments of the rock which are broken off by the rope...'

Climmer going over the cliff

The eccentric Squire Waterton was delighted by his own experience:

'The sea was roaring at the base of the stupendous wall of rocks; thousands and tens of thousands of wildfowl were in an instant on the wing... The nests of the kittiwakes were close to each other, on every part of the rocks that was capable of holding them and they were so numerous as totally to defy any attempt to count them.'

In Waterton's day up to 130,000 eggs could be collected in the season. They were sold for different purposes. Some were turned into souvenirs, some were used for sugar refining and some sent to the West Riding where the egg white was used in the manufacture of patent leather. But most were eaten by local people who cooked up guillemot egg omelettes and other similar delectables.

The Seabird Preservation Act 1869 was passed to stop the slaughter of the birds by visiting Victorian shooting parties, and The Wild Birds Protection Act 1954, which made the taking of wild birds' eggs illegal, put an end to legal 'climming'.

WORTHY OF HIS HIRE

Whilst fishing was always a dominant occupation along the coast, farming also provided employment for many youngsters when they reached working age. Both boys and girls could start their working lives from as young as 12 or 13.

In the 19th and early 20th centuries, one annual event along the coast, and indeed across the whole of the East Riding, was the Martinmas Hirings where those looking for work on farms gathered.

For farm lads, life on the farm was a notoriously hard regime, starting in the early morning and finishing when the work was done, toiling for six days of the week and for 51 weeks a year. The hired lads lived in, either with the farmer or farm foreman whose 'missus' looked after them. It was her cooking and generosity of provision that often determined the good reputation of the farmer. The lads expected (and needed) three good meals a day and the best housewives offered meat, veggies, pies (both savoury and sweet) and probably a whole lot more beside to satisfy the appetites of growing lads.

Living conditions were pretty rough; often the lads would be crowded together in an attic or granary – sweltering in summer and freezing in winter. There were few, if any, washing facilities save a pump or cold tap in the farmyard or outside the kitchen door.

Farm servants' contracts ran for one year from Martinmas Day (November 11th). These contracts were unwritten, based on local custom and practice and virtually unbreakable on either side. Wages were not paid until the end of the year and as they were handed out, anyone well-regarded by the farmer would be asked to stay on for another year. Mostly the lads moved on but whether they stayed or not depended on how they viewed their treatment during the year, for some farmers were bad masters.

Those lads that did leave their 'spot' took themselves off to the nearest market town where the annual hiring fair was held. All spruced up and dressed in their best, they stood in the market place, preening and parading a little self-consciously to show themselves off to the farmers, who walked up and down assessing and questioning those offering their services. A servant was engaged for the coming year, after a bout of bargaining had settled the wage, by a handshake and the acceptance of a 'fastener' which at various times ranged from a penny to a shilling. If the coin was not returned by the end of the day, then a legal contract had been established which could not be broken.

On our coast, both Bridlington and Hornsea held hiring fairs where bargains were struck and men hired by the payment of the 'fastener'. Normally there was more than one fair held in the week following Martinmas Day. Hirings have received a bad press in the past, being portrayed as akin to slave auctions. However, in Holderness and the East Riding as a whole, they were open, public affairs which stymied any employer looking to skew the market or establish a monopoly. There were usually sufficient jobs for all of those seeking work and a bad farmer/employer found it hard to hire anyone as word soon got around.

The hirings were the only time the farm servants had a holiday and once the main business was done, they made the most of it. The hiring towns were crowded with folk, especially young people, all ready to party and eager to have a good time.

With a year's wages rattling in pockets, there was shopping to be done, friends to catch up with, debts to be paid and scores to be settled in any handy dark alley. The towns' shopkeepers did a roaring trade as did the pubs. After a year, isolated on the farm, seeing the same faces day in, day out, the opportunity to let off a bit of steam was too good to miss. When the hirings took place a funfair usually came to town as well to add to the week's excitement.

The hirings system continued into the early years of the 20th century until changes in farming practices, increased mechanisation and the introduction of more formal bargaining and regulation through wages committees brought the system to a close and ended a way of life which on the whole had served communities, families and individuals well.

A COLLECTION OF COBBLES

One requirement for a coastal dweller (in addition to stoic resilience in the face of the sea's relentless appetite for *terra firma*) was a certain sort of resourcefulness — the ability to make the most of all the natural resources around.

An abundant natural resource to be found everywhere along the coast lay on the beaches — that of building material — and an important source of work on the coastal strip was the collection of this material, particularly cobbles, gravel and sand from the beaches. From the 18th century onwards these materials were used not only for building but also for making roads and to provide ballast for ships.

The cobbles were gathered from the eroding boulder clay of the cliffs and the frequency of the erosion produced an equally constant supply. The cobbles varied in rock type, some having clearly travelled a long way during the glacial melt at the end of the last Ice Age.

Technically, only those owning shore rights — usually the Lord of the Manor — could remove material from the beaches.

Normally though, said owners licensed others to do the grafting and received royalties for the removal of the material.

In the 1860s a bit of a spat arose between Sir Thomas Constable and the Lady of the Manor of Mappleton and Cowden about shore rights. Sir Thomas won the day and licensed three men in Aldbrough to remove cobbles at 6d per ton and eight men at Cowden toiled at a rate of 3d per ton. In addition, the men had to buy a licence from Sir Thomas at a cost of between £2 and £8.

All along the coast men worked in this trade until the work of collecting the cobbles developed on a large scale. Our tireless hiker, Walter White observed whilst walking on the beach near Atwick in 1860:

'Looking inland... everywhere a path zigzags up you will notice large trays used for carrying up the heaps of pebbles there accumulated, for the construction of drains, fences, and walls.'
A Month in Yorkshire, 1861

Donkeys saddled with two panniers were often used to carry the cobbles off the beach and at Cowden for example, a landing point was built to bring the materials up from the beach. The cobbles were then moved on and delivered overland or by boat.

Not surprisingly with such a handy building material, many of the local cottages, farms, barns, wall and even some churches are built from the cobbles, their builders creating interesting variations and patterns. In Easington for example there are cottages whose walls are built from the cobbles in the form of herringbone patterns. In other places the cobbles are fairly randomly placed. Occasionally the cobbles are mixed in with locally made brick which is used to frame squares of cobbles. There are probably few other building materials so rustic and attractive yet, given their random round shapes, so difficult to work with.

Gathering cobbles at Atwick

The industry became such an extensive one that concerns began to be raised about the part played in erosion by the removal not only of cobbles, but also of sand and gravel. A ban on removing material from the beaches between Atwick and Spurn was put in place in 1869 but every now and then, at night, illicit loads were hauled away.

Walter White found that at least one person bemoaned the ban – the landlady of a pub at Spurn Head:

'... She has but few guests now, and talks with regret of the change since the digging of ballast was forbidden on the Spurn. Then trade was good, for the diggers were numerous and thirsty.'

Nevertheless, he at least did seem to have some appreciation of the damage the trade caused:

'That ballast-digging should ever have been permitted in so unstable a spot argues a great want of forethought somewhere.'

'BRANDY FOR THE PARSON, 'BACCY FOR THE CLERK'

Living on the Holderness coast, caught in the battle between land and sea did not make earning the daily crust an easy business. Small wonder then that private, duty-free enterprise, otherwise known as smuggling, attracted many otherwise law-abiding citizens.

The 18th century was a golden age for smuggling in England and any coastal area appears to have involved itself in the trade when a man could earn his daily bread and much more from a packhorse load of merchandise than he could from a week's wage. One contemporary writer asserts, *'some of the farmers found more profit in navigating to and fro with smuggled merchandise concealed under loads of hay and barley than in cultivating their farms.'*

The Holderness coast is just a hop and a skip away from Holland across the cold and grey North Sea facilitating this brisk export and import business, and the wide flat Holderness beaches are made for discreet, remote landings on a still, dark night. There was a small sloop based at Bridlington known to make regular crossings over the North Sea to a port in Zeeland, Holland. This sloop routinely landed its cargo of tea, tobacco and gin at places on the coast between Spurn point and Bridlington and probably in quantities vastly exceeding the meagre duty-free allowances of today.

Large boats called coopers, bristling with guns, hove-to off shore like floating cash-and-carry warehouses whereupon local folk from the Holderness villages would venture out in smaller boats to acquire merchandise for further distribution to friends, family and valued customers. Their boats were often adapted for the purpose with false bulkheads or a *paillasse* stuffed with tea and tobacco. Cargoes were also regularly run up the River Humber to be met by ships coming down from the River Ouse ready to take the goodies further inland.

It was the job of the revenue men (assisted by the navy) to prevent smuggling, and intercept and capture the smugglers at sea. It was not a popular career and the revenue men had a hard time of it. In 1701 the Yorkshire Customs Force was increased, although in comparison to the numbers of people involved in the trade, they were outnumbered. A customs officer is quoted as saying, '*show me a fisherman and I will show you a smuggler*'. It was no sinecure to be a customs officer – they were a most unloved species – abused, mocked, assaulted and even murdered.

In 1777 Captain Mitchell of the revenue cutter *Swallow* met a notorious smuggler called Stoney in his schooner *Kent*. Captain Mitchell sent in this report of the encounter:

'*as their* [the Kent] *guns were in readiness, and at the same time waving us to go to the Northward, we were, by reason of their superior force, obliged to sheer off, but did our best endeavours to spoil his Market.*'

This was not the first time that Captain Mitchell decided it was better to render himself able to 'fight another day'; he was either very prudent or very timorous and perhaps not without cause. Despite the romantic view presented in fiction, smugglers were dangerous, ruthless and violent men.

At the most northerly tip of the coast, the caves in the cliffs at Flamborough Head offered first class storage facilities for contraband and in the 18th and 19th centuries tea, brandy, tobacco, silk and cotton were, by various sneaky means, smuggled ashore under the noses of the excise men. A notorious smuggler, Robin Lythe is reputed to have used the caves, but then that might just be a tale for the tourist trade.

At one time there was no resident vicar of the church in Hornsea, only a curate who visited now and again to save the souls of Hornsea dwellers. Without the regular presence of a churchman, the parish clerk, clearly a man of enterprise, conceived the idea of storing contraband in the crypt of the church. On Christmas Eve 1732, perhaps in anticipation of the festivities, he opened the door to the crypt just at the moment when the town was struck by a hurricane. Since hurricanes are not the norm in these northern parts some might consider that Him (or Her) 'Up There' was not best pleased at the use to which His (or Her) House was put. Whatever the case, the hurricane ripped the roof off the church and at the same time as it went flying away, the clerk keeled over. One correspondent wrote later that the man was, *'afflicted with a paralytic stroke which deprived him of the use of his speech and confined him to bed for some months before his death.'*

In the letter describing this event it is clear that certain of the townsfolk were aware that a well-known smuggler and his ship were close by at Hornsea Beck and that the sudden hurricane-esque storm laid flat his ship. Apart from knowing the smuggler was called George we know little more or even whether free-enterprising Hornsea folk enjoyed a pipe of baccy and a glass of brandy that Christmas – all duty free of course.

Revenue cutter chasing a smuggling lugger by Charles Dixon RI
(1872-1934)

Chapter Five
For Those In Peril on the Sea

Those who live and work on the Holderness coast know only too well the dangers to be faced when storms blow up, seas surge and treacherous tides put lives and ships at risk. The seabed is littered with wrecks; along the southern half of the coast alone, between Aldbrough and Spurn Point, at least 500 shipwrecks have been recorded.

It was an unusual year that did not see several casualties somewhere along the coast and such events often involved the ships being driven ashore by gales and strong tides and wrecked in the process. The rights to take and sell any wreckage or cargos that washed up on the beaches was often held by the Lord of the Manor or gifted to one of the church or monastic landowners on the coast. In Mappleton for example, the typically square and solid Norman church tower was embellished with a pointy steeple built from stone ballast from a shipwreck and the village joiner's shop was adorned with nameplates garnered from the wreckage of ships lost off the coast there.

Joiner's shop in Mappleton showing nameplates of lost ships

One of the better known wrecks is that of the *Earl of Beaconsfield*, a four-masted, iron sailing barque. She started life as *Cuba*, a three-masted passenger steamer of the Cunard Line in 1864 and made her maiden voyage from Liverpool to New York in December of that year. She continued to make the Atlantic crossing until 1876 when Cunard decided she was too small to be economical (carrying 160 passengers) and she was sold to Brown's of London. She was subsequently converted to a four-mast sailing ship and renamed the *Earl of Beaconsfield* after Queen Victoria's favourite Prime Minister. In 1877 the ship made a record run from London to Hudson Bay in 78 days.

In 1887 whilst bringing a cargo of linseed and wheat from Calcutta she foundered in thick fog onto a sandbank off the coast near Aldbrough. Three tugs were brought out to assist her and tow her off but as the weather deteriorated, it was to no avail. Her 37 crew members were taken off the ship by the lifeboat. The ship was valued at £25,000 and her cargo at £35,000 – no mean sums in those days.

After she foundered, she was put to good use by the local bird population. In a book, *The Birds of Yorkshire* by T H Nelson published in 1907, it was recorded that cormorants:

'... appropriated on the wreck of a sailing ship, the "Earl of Beaconsfield," that went ashore near Aldbrough in 1887. One of the masts is left standing to warn fishing cobles of the danger to navigation, and on the crosstrees of the main mast several pairs of Cormorants have established themselves; in 1893 it was reported that a pair had nested and brought off young, and since then they have been regularly observed; sixteen were seen on 31st August 1900, and nestlings have been recognised. In winter some return to the ship at sunset, but in early autumn they are "at home" after the tide begins to

flow, when contests frequently take place for the post of honour.'

Today, her bows can be seen at low tide and her stern lies just a few feet under water, and she proves a popular dive site.

The figurehead from the *Earl of Beaconsfield* was retrieved by a local family and finally handed over to the Hull Maritime Museum where it is now restored and on display.

Figurehead of the *Earl of Beaconsfield*

THE *SILVERDALE* AND *STRATON* COLLISION

The *Earl of Beaconsfield* was lost in fog and foul weather. However even in favourable conditions disaster may strike, as happened in the collision between the steam trawlers SS *Silverdale* and SS *Straton*.

It was just three weeks into the New Year of 1911 when the steam trawler SS *Silverdale* left the Port of Grimsby heading for the North Sea fishing grounds with nine hands on board. A few days later, with a full catch in her hold, she began her homeward voyage, arriving off Spurn Point early in the morning of February 4th. There she stopped for about an hour and waited for the tide. The weather was fine and clear, the sea was smooth.

Members of the *Silverdale* crew observed lights from other ships around this busy seaway where vessels made for the ports of Hull and Grimsby. Shortly after getting underway again to complete the last leg of their voyage back to Grimsby, they suddenly heard blasts from a warning whistle and almost immediately after there was a loud crash. The *Silverdale* shuddered as the trawler *Straton* struck her amidships.

In the dark confusion that follows the skipper George Grice shouts at the other trawler that the *Silverdale* is sinking and to come about for a rescue; Frank Foster, the chief engineer, knocked off his feet in the collision, picks himself up and staggers onto deck calling out that the engine room is full of water. He and the mate, John Walling try to release the lifeboat but the stern of the *Silverdale* sinks quickly, in the space of just a couple of minutes and they find themselves in the freezing waters along with the other members of the crew.

At the subsequent Court of Inquiry, the captain of the *Straton*, Daniel Jacob Joenson, stated he and his ship were returning from a voyage to the Faroes and heading homewards. When the ship arrived off Withernsea the captain laid up there until around 4 am when he gave the order to get the ship underway again, steaming at slow ahead. As the vessel approached Spurn he saw the lights of the *Silverdale* some half to a mile off and left the shelter of the wheelhouse to check his own side and masthead lights which he found to be burning brightly. On returning to the wheelhouse he noticed that the *Silverdale* lights were showing much nearer and the vessel was on a course heading straight for the *Straton*. He sounded the warning whistle and, at the same time, rang down instructions to the engine room for full speed astern. However there was only just time to thrust the ship into reverse before the two vessels collided.

After the collision, the *Straton* re-bounded from the *Silverdale* and, after checking the damage to his own vessel, Joenson brought her about to look for survivors; other trawlers nearby steamed to the rescue alerted by the crew of the *Spurn Lightship* who sent up rockets and fired guns to attract their attention.

Of the *Silverdale*'s original nine-man crew only four survivors – Foster and Walling, together with deck hand Robert Hicks who floated in the water clinging to a lifebuoy and James Wright the steward who hung on to a deck fish pound board – were picked up.

Of those lost, the skipper was last seen heading for the wheelhouse and was presumed to have gone down with his ship and the four other crew members clung to wreckage for a short while but sadly succumbed to exhaustion and the dark, icy cold waters of the North Sea before they could be rescued.

The inquiry concluded that both vessels, to different degrees had failed to comply with the Regulations for the Prevention of Collisions at Sea and that the *Silverdale* was not 'navigated with proper and seamanlike care'. Despite some strictures laid upon the captain of the *Straton,* the court held the opinion that the loss of the Silverdale and some of its crew members was not caused by any 'wrongful act or default of the skipper of the *Straton*'.

Lighting the Way

The waters around Spurn Point and the Humber estuary became increasingly busy as the ports of Hull, Grimsby and later Immingham developed, leading to a greater need for navigation assistance to keep ships and seamen safe. Before technology improved and developed, lighthouses played a significant role in keeping mariners safe at sea. They aided navigation and marked dangerous coastlines, shoals and reefs.

Along the Holderness coast there were three lighthouses, only one of which still functions.

Lighthouses and Liquor

At the southernmost tip of the coast lies Spurn Point where the tides of the cold inhospitable waters of the North Sea quarrel with those of the River Humber. Lighthouses have existed here since medieval times when the lost port of Ravenser existed. The first lighthouse, built in 1360, is recorded as only the third one to be built in the British Isles.

Engineer John Smeaton became involved with Spurn in 1767. By this time the previous pair of lighthouses, built by Justinian Angell around 1674 had, through the shifting of Spurn's sands, become so far inland of the Point as to be a danger to shipping.

Smeaton submitted drawings to Trinity House for two lighthouses and two temporary ones. At the time it was customary to build pairs of lighthouses known as the lower light and the upper light. This approach enabled ships' captains to take bearings off each light and so fix a position. Trinity House approved Smeaton's drawings and temporary lights were built in summer 1767. Leonard Thompson of York built them and revenue from the charges paid by passing ships were split between him and John Angell whose family held a grant of land at Spurn.

The contract to build Smeaton's permanent lights was a difficult one to let. Spurn was (and is) remote, access difficult, weather uncertain and entertainment for the staff non-existent. Eventually Trinity House awarded a contract to the lowest priced contractor, William Taylor, in April 1770. The following year Smeaton took up his appointment as Surveyor of Works. In that twelvemonth the sea had nibbled away at the eastern side of Spurn shifting it somewhat and necessitating a change in the position of the lower light. Work began on the foundations for this lower light using timber piles driven deep into the spit. Once these were in place in July 1773 the rest of the lighthouse was built and finished some six months later.

Spurn Lighthouse

The upper light became a victim of a dispute between the Angell family and the Constable family, the wealthy Holderness landowners mentioned previously. Building work was suspended for a year whilst they squabbled over who owned what and who did what to whom. Eventually though the foundations were laid. Four concentric circles of wood piles were driven in to a depth of over 2 metres, then topped off with a stone platform approximately 30 cm thick. The upper light towered a full 27.4 metres high and was built in brick.

The building of the lighthouses brought new faces to this remote spot. Taylor the builder leased a house and applied for a licence to sell liquor. He had a rival licensee though, the lighthouse keeper, John Foster. It was not an unusual occurrence for people working along this remote coast to have two or even three employments; the very first lighthouse keeper on Spurn was also a licensee selling liquor to men from visiting ships.

Conflict ensued between Foster and Taylor and on one occasion Foster is said to have thrown burning coals over one of Taylor's workmen. However difficult it was to keep labour in such a remote spot, filling them full of booze was not the answer. Taylor was clearly lacking somewhat in man-management skills and the work just did not get done. Smeaton wrote, sorrowfully if rather naively, that he believed that once the men got drunk at the lighthouse keepers establishment, *'they seldom go to work anymore'*.

In 1776 a heavy storm exposed the low light's foundations and Smeaton needed to take remedial action. Nevertheless both lights were ready to be shown off in September 1776 when local stone coal which burns bright and white was used for the lamps. Smeaton certified final completion of both lights in 1777 when he commented on one site visit that although, *'the brick-work of both houses is somewhat rough ... I have no doubt of the firmness of the work'*.

For more than a century Smeaton's lights burned brightly until the upper light was replaced, making the lower light superfluous. In the 1980s new technology and techniques diminished the need for some lighthouses and on the night of October 31st 1985, Spurn's bright warning light swept across the Humber and the North Sea for the last time.

At the northernmost tip of the Holderness coast lies Flamborough Head – a chalk headland whose sheer white cliffs thrust out into the North Sea. On the cliff top stand two lighthouse towers, the first dating to 1669 and the second, the Flamborough Head Lighthouse, built in 1806 and still in use today.

The first light was built by Sir John Clayton. Apart from the Flamborough light, he and his partner George Blake proposed to build others at Foulness, Cromer, the Farne Islands and Corton near Lowestoft in Suffolk.

In 1669 Clayton received a government patent for the four sites. The patent lasted for 60 years and provided for specific charges to be paid to the two partners by the owners of passing vessels. Work began and Clayton and his Partner completed Flamborough in 1669 at a cost of £3,000.

However there was just one snag. Instead of the light illuminating the sky, the whole project fizzled out and it was never lit – probably because, as they found at the other sites, it was too costly to service the light. The anticipated income never materialised as the charges set out in the patent were only to be paid voluntarily or as generally happened, not at all. However, it is the oldest surviving complete lighthouse in England.

The present lighthouse, designed by Samuel Wyatt, cost £8,000 to build and its lamp was first lit on December 1st 1806. The tower itself tops 25 metres and the lamp rises 65 metres above a typical high water. The original lighting setup was an innovative design using red glass covered reflectors to create the characteristic two white followed by one red flash signal. This colourful display distinguished Flamborough from the Cromer Lighthouse further south on the Norfolk coast. The lighthouse was conceived as a guide for coasters and ships from the Baltic and North Sea and continues to be a marker for deep sea ships and coastal traffic, as well as vessels heading for local ports such as Bridlington. It was automated in 1996.

The First Flamborough Lighthouse

STUCK IN THE MIDDLE

The town of Withernsea hugs the coast roughly halfway between Flamborough and Spurn point. Today, if you drive down one of its main streets you will be confronted by a towering white, octagonal edifice rising incongruously from the middle of housing and shops. It is the Withernsea Lighthouse.

Withernsea Lighthouse

It was built around 1892 a quarter of a mile back from the coast but what then intervened between it and the sea were sand dunes and a mere. Nevertheless, it was chosen as the site for good reason – there were a high number of shipwrecks off Withernsea because vessels could not see the lights of either Spurn or Flamborough and so floundered about. The Withernsea lighthouse provided a much needed point of reference and a means of protecting the town's pier which took a starring role in many shipwrecks and collisions.

The lighthouse has no separate floors, just 144 wheeze-inducing spiral staircase steps leading to the lamp room at the top. The original paraffin lamp (eight wicks no less) was housed in an octagonal revolving two-ton lens and that floated in a trough containing three gallons of mercury. The mechanism that turned the lens needed daily winding by hand until that task became superfluous when the whole shebang was electrified. Withernsea lighthouse continued to warn ships away from its pier until, as a venerable 82-year-old, it beamed its last in 1976.

A NOBLE ENDEAVOUR

When all else failed and a vessel got into difficulty it was the bravery and determination of the lifeboat crews, coastguards and rocket men that saved lives – just as it is today. Headstones in graveyards up and down the coast remind us that in saving many, some are lost. This is the story of the day of February 10th 1871 when a violent gale tested the courage of all who went to assist ships and sailors in distress.

For several days earlier the weather had been atrocious and ships huddled in the shelter of ports higher up the coast on Tyneside and Teeside. When a break in the weather occurred, a large convoy of ships left shelter and headed south. However, the westerly wind that helped them on their way dropped suddenly on the evening of February 9th and many ships were becalmed in Bridlington Bay. In the early hours of the morning of February 10th the wind got up, increasing in strength all the while and bringing sleet and snow with it until it turned into a vicious ice-storm. It also changed direction and blew from the south-east straight into Bridlington Bay and in doing so bottled up many of the becalmed ships.

As soon as grey morning light broke, lifeboats, rocket apparatus and all their crews were readied. It was obvious that many of the ships were in great danger. Some masters tried to run their ships ashore for safety; others, choosing to ride out the storm, were driven mercilessly onto the shore by the huge waves and boiling surf. Bit by bit, with anchors dragging behind them, 17 ships were thrown ashore to be pounded and smashed up by mountainous waves.

Both Bridlington lifeboats were launched and the rocket crews assembled. The local coastguards swam or waded chest-high through turbulent surf to pull crews off the nearer wrecks and get them to safety. Townsfolk ran to the sea walls to help out wherever they could.

The lifeboat *Robert Whitworth* went out time after time to the wrecks, snatching the sailors from certain death. In one case its crew fought for two hours to reach a vessel but was repeatedly beaten back. On returning to harbour, exhausted crew members were lifted from the boat with hands raw and bleeding from the oars. By this time conditions were so dangerous the *Robert Whitworth* was withdrawn from service, having saved 12 lives.

Meanwhile the other Bridlington lifeboat, the *Harbinger*, put out to sea again and again and as one crewman fell exhausted another stepped forward to take his place. However, after the seventh launch, during which sailors from another four vessels were safely recovered, replacement crew were becoming difficult to find. At this point it appeared that the *Harbinger*, like the *Robert Whitworth,* would have to be withdrawn.

However when David Purdon, *Harbinger's* builder and John Clappison, his assistant, stepped up and volunteered to take her out, another seven men came forward to help. They set off to rescue the crew of the brig *Delta*, aground and breaking up on Wilsthorpe Sands. However, on the way they came across another grounded vessel and took off the five man crew, landed them and then turned back to the brig. When they finally got there they found only one crew member, the captain, clinging desperately to the rigging. All the others had taken to the brig's lifeboat and drowned when it capsized.

Just as the *Harbinger* hove alongside the *Delta* a tremendous wave struck the brig sending her crashing into the lifeboat. The lifeboat, hit by the same wave, was thrown into the air and turned turtle. For a few minutes the *Harbinger* remained upside down until another wave righted her. One crewman, Richard Bedlington remained in the boat and he helped another, John Robinson, to climb back in, using his scarf as a rope. One further crew member, Richard Hopper, managed to scramble back aboard. The six other lifeboat crew all perished, including the first two volunteers David Purdon and John Clappison. All the boat's oars were lost or smashed and eventually the boat drifted ashore near Wilsthorpe.

As the day wore on the destruction and loss of life continued as it became almost impossible to launch rescues, though not for want of trying. Those on shore could only watch helplessly as men struggled for their lives. A contemporary report describes how, *'the piercing cries of the drowning crews were frequently heard amidst the howling of the storm'*.

All through the night distress signals were seen far out at sea but by daybreak on February 11th the wind dropped and the devastation of the storm was revealed. Debris, timber spars, coal and wood littered the beaches amongst the wreckage of the vessels. Estimates put the number of ships lost to be around 30; the exact number of lives lost is not known but generally estimated at around 70. Corpses were still washed ashore two weeks after the storm.

On February 14th the first mass funeral took place of three captains, 19 crew and James Watson a crewman from the *Harbinger*. An estimated 4,000 people turned out to pay their respects. A public fund was set up to assist the widows and orphans of those lost as well as those who manned the lifeboats. Public subscriptions also paid for a monument erected over the mass grave at Priory Churchyard in Bridlington in memory of all those lost. The inscriptions serve to remind us of the price paid that terrible day. On one side of the monument the inscription gives the names of those lost, *'whilst nobly endeavouring to save those whose bodies rest below'*. The other three sides contain inscriptions, *'in lasting memory of a great company of Seamen who perished in the fearful gale… on February 10th 1871'*, listing the names and number of ships lost before finishing with the grim tally, *'Forty-three bodies of those who on that day lost their lives, lie in this churchyard'*.

All Calm on Wilsthorpe Sands Today

Chapter Six
A Call to Arms

The Holderness coast has always offered would-be conquerors open landing places providing captains could navigate the shoals and manage the tides and currents. Over the centuries, in times of invasion and war, the normally sleepy Holderness coast woke up.

The lost ports of Ravenser and Ravenser Odd saw the arrival of kings and wanna-be kings. Henry Bolingbroke landed at Ravenser in 1399. He did not tarry to chat to the natives, so intent was he on dethroning Richard II.

Residents not taking part in the battle for the English throne would observe a little local resistance led by Sir Martin De La See against Edward IV's landing on March 14th 1471 when he blagged his way back into the country on the pretence of paying family visits.

Earlier, the townsfolk of Ravenser Odd supported Kings Edward II and III in their wars against Scotland, providing men, arms and supplies for the fight.

This chapter describes events from five wars, across five centuries that in some way, large or small, affected the lives of those living along the coast. We start with the 16th century and the Spanish Armada before looking in on the English Civil War, The American War of Independence, the Napoleonic Wars and concluding with the First World War.

THE SPANIARDS ARE COMING

Despite the remote nature of the Holderness Coast one scrap of news that must have made headline news in markets and taverns up and down the coast was the war with Spain and the coming of the Spanish Armada in 1588. All along the coast from Spurn Point in the south to Flamborough in the north a series of warning beacons was set up. Aldbrough, Mappleton, Hornsea, Skipsea and Barmston formed part of this early warning system. Each village had three beacons made up from tar barrels set on high stakes and zealously guarded 24 hours a day, seven days a week.

The job description for the role of beacon watchman ran something like this:

Role Title:	Day Watchman (2 vacancies) Night Watchman (3 vacancies)

Main Tasks:	In conjunction with colleagues, to:
	• Watch out for ships at sea or in the river Humber.
	• Determine whether the ships' actions, course changes or anything else give suspicion that they might do harm on land.
	• Light the beacons according to the given code:
	  - one barrel to be lit for spying anything suspicious;
	  - two barrels if a number of ships together were seen as these might be part of the enemy fleet;
	  - all three barrels to be lit should the enemy have landed.

Personal Characteristics required:	• Good eyesight (especially night vision for the Night Watchmen posts). • Wisdom, discretion, honesty. • Fit and able to run very fast when necessary. Must be a householder over thirty.

These coastal beacons were linked to others further inland whose watchmen picked up the baton as it were and passed on the warning message. Local churches could no longer toll their bells and call to the faithful; now they could only peal if and when an emergency arose. Meanwhile, country folk were instructed to drive all livestock and remove all victuals further inland, to deny them to the enemy.

The plan for the defence of the realm included the notion that in coastal areas local militia would respond to any initial landing and inland militia would form the next line of defence. It is interesting to speculate what type of defence force our coastal locals would have made.

For example in Hornsea the number of fighting men amounted to about 40, comprising pike, bill and musket men together with a couple of archers. The town's armoury might just have produced enough to clothe and arm one and a half men, although which half is debatable. Fortunately, although local people may have glimpsed part of the Spanish fleet as it fled up the east coast to Scotland, these arrangements for the defence of the realm were never actually put to the test.

A FUNDRAISING ROYALIST

The 17th century heralded the English Civil War – those austere, fun-hating, round-headed Puritans versus the dashing, gay, curly-wigged Cavaliers. But nothing is ever as simple as a dispute over headwear – several factors contributed to the conflict; two different interpretations of the same faith – Protestantism; the principle of the Divine Right of Kings to rule willy-nilly; growing aggravation between town and country and between ordinary people and gentry. The war split families, setting fathers against sons and brothers against brothers.

The war came close to our coastal villages and particularly on the southern edge around the villages of Kilnsea and Easington. Villagers would soon hear that the men of the city of

Hull had slammed the gates shut in the face of the King Charles I and would have wondered if trouble was heading their way. Similarly, when Sir John Meldrum brought 1,500 troops by sea to secure the port of Hull for parliament, the sight of a flotilla of ships heading up the estuary would not have passed unnoticed and un-gossiped about by those on the southern edges of the coast.

The war also placed unlikely people in unusual situations. Take for example Queen Henrietta Maria, the Catholic wife of the English King, Charles I.

In 1642, when civil war looked a certainty, Henrietta Maria left England for the Netherlands where she busied herself as a good wife should by raising money, buying weapons and recruiting troops for the Royalist cause. Braving storms at sea she returned to England, landing in Bridlington Bay in February 1643. Two days after her arrival five warships commanded by Parliamentarian Admiral Batten sailed into the bay at night and had the temerity to open fire with their cannon on the houses along the quayside where the Queen lodged. In a letter to the King, the Queen wrote:

'One of their ships did me the favour of flanking on the house where I slept and before I was out of bed the balls whished so loud about me that my company pressed me earnestly to go out of the house.'

Once persuaded to leave, the Queen, her ladies-in-waiting, her dog Mitte – a King Charles spaniel of course – and her dwarf Sir Jeffrey Hudson retired to the safety of a most un-regal ditch some distance away. She continued her letter:

'So, clothed as well as in haste I could be, I went on foot to some little distance from the town of Burlington [Bridlington] and got in the shelter of a ditch, whither before I could get, the cannon balls fell thick about us, and a servant was killed within

seventy paces of me. One dangerous ball grazed the edge of the ditch and covered us with earth and stones.'

Whilst Her Royal Highness was being thus bombarded, William Cavendish, was halfway en route to the coast to escort her to Beverley and sent his cavalry swiftly ahead to ensure the Queen's safety. He followed these troops with his infantry as fast as he could. Meanwhile, the Parliamentarian warships letting fly at poor Bridlington were quickly sent packing by the approach of the Dutch fleet under Van Tromp.

Brave Henrietta Maria was not amused by this attack on her royal personage and prosed on about the incident at length both to William and later the king. However, her arrival was welcome and provided something of a relief for the Royalists as she brought with her 1,000 Royalist volunteers, enough supplies to fill 250 wagons and £80,000 in gold. All in all, it was probably reckoned to be worth a night spent in a ditch at the expense of a little royal dignity.

'SURRENDER – I HAVE NOT YET BEGUN TO FIGHT!'

Roll forward the years to the next century and the American War of Independence. In 1778-79 in the waters around Britain, American privateer John Paul Jones – pirate or hero depending on which side you favour – was doing what he could to harass and capture commercial shipping. In addition he added to the embarrassment of one of the Marshals of the Admiralty, William Brough, whose unenviable task it was to suppress piracy in the area. Brough lived in the village of Rolston just south of Hornsea and half a mile from the coast. Whenever JP sailed up the Holderness coast, as he went by the cliffs bordering Rolston, he would render 'passing honours' to Mr Brough by firing a cannon ball at Rolston Hall, Brough's home.

At this time the coast was on high alert and men from the Northumberland Militia were billeted along it at Bridlington,

Skipsea, Hornsea and Mappleton. In Bridlington the militia was called out as soon as JP's fleet was spied to prevent him from landing as he had done elsewhere on his travels.

The Battle of Flamborough Head took place on September 23rd 1779 and despite its small scale, the engagement became one of the most celebrated naval actions of the American War of Independence and marked the founding of the American Navy.

JP's squadron consisted of three ships which had been lurking off Spurn Point looking for prizes to capture as ships left the Humber. He decided to sail north up the Holderness coast and just off Flamborough Head, he spotted a convoy of around 40 ships returning from the Baltic. On spying JP's ships, the merchant shipping made for the safety of Scarborough further up the coast protected by a small armed vessel the *Countess of Scarborough*. The other escort ship was the Royal Navy frigate, *Serapis,* which, commanded by Captain Richard Pearson, turned to engage the American at around six o'clock that evening.

The main battle was between the *Serapis* and JP's ship, the *Bonhomme Richard*. After exchanging fire at long range, the two ships closed in on each other, collided and became hopelessly entangled – locked together side by side and neither ship able to move. At this point Captain Pearson asked JP whether his ship had struck (surrendered) to which JP is alleged to have uttered his immortal words, *'Surrender... I have not yet begun to fight!'*. Pearson pounded the hull of the *Bonhomme* at close quarters and JP placed men in the rigging to release murderous fire at the sailors on the *Serapis* decks below. Attempts by both sides to board the other's enemy ship were repulsed.

The *Serapis, b*y Robert Dodd (1748–1815)

The battle raged for four hours and both ships were badly mauled; JP's ship was holed below the waterline and fire broke out several times on both vessels. Sometime after 10 o'clock in the evening, another ship from JP's squadron joined the fray and as fire neared the powder magazine on the *Serapis*, Pearson, knowing the convoy (which was his main duty) was safe, struck his colours.

JP reluctantly abandoned his own ship – by now listing badly, on fire and ready to go under – and transferred to the captured *Serapis*.

The following day, having seen Pearson and what was left of his crew (both sides lost about half their crews during the battle) to safety, JP put a crew aboard the *Bonhomme* to try and save her, but in vain. The *Bonhomme Richard* sank in Bridlington Bay at 11 o'clock that morning.

In recognition of their endeavours Pearson and his officers were honoured by the towns of Hull and Scarborough and rewarded by the Russia Company, the main owners of the vessels in the commercial convoy.

In writing his account of the battle to the Admiralty and announcing the capture of his ship, Captain Pearson wrote,

'I flatter myself with the hopes that their lordships will be convinced that she has not been given away.'

Clearly their lordships concurred and Captain Pearson was knighted in 1780 and they were sufficiently impressed as to launch a new *Serapis* some years later – a somewhat unusual occurrence because normally when a ship lost a battle its name was seldom revived.

GRIMSTON'S CAVALRY RIDES TO WAR

The latter years of the 18th and the first of the 19th century saw Britain's struggle against Napoleon Bonaparte. Whilst most of the fighting took place in Portugal, Spain and France itself, nevertheless the call to action was heard along the Holderness coast. The military commander at the time in issuing his call to action said:

'that the coast of Holderness which lies so immediately exposed to the Enemy should be Put into such a state of Preparation for defence as under the Divine Protection may render ineffectual and finally defeat every attempt on the Part of our Inveterate Enemies.'

The threat of a French invasion loomed large and so bigwigs in the East Riding set about raising companies of volunteers to swell the military numbers. In 1794 at a meeting in Beverley a number of measures were proposed for the defence of the Holderness coast, including:

- The fort at Bridlington Quay be repaired and the Government requested to supply ordnance and ammunition.
- A company of infantry be raised to man the fort.
- One corps of cavalry be raised, not exceeding 50.

The Lord Lieutenant of the East Riding suggested that:

'It might be expedient to begin immediately to raise two companies at nearly the extremities of our Coast, namely Bridlington and Patrington... It might likewise be desirable to have a third company stationed in a more central situation for instance at Hornsey.' [Hornsea]

Thus, at Bridlington John Pitts put together a group of volunteer gunners to man the fort guns and a company of infantry to guard the coast. On the southern end of the coast, William Raines formed a volunteer infantry. In the middle Digby Ledgard was tasked with mustering a company for Hornsea. Unfortunately, the menfolk of Hornsea failed to hear or heed the call and only two recruits were forthcoming. The centre of the coast would have been left defenceless had it not been for the sterling efforts of Thomas Grimston of Grimston Hall who, at his own expense, raised a cavalry force.

He rode tirelessly up and down the coast as well as inland Holderness trying to stir the patriotic zeal of the locals and entice them to join his cavalry force. Unfortunately, his rousing words and ambitious plans fell on deaf ears. Acting on the principle, 'if at first you don't succeed...' he persuaded the local clergy to call parish meetings so that the importance and purpose of the proposed cavalry could be clearly explained to the bashful locals. Once more Grimston was disappointed. In a letter explaining this lack of local patriotism he was told:

'what they object to is the smallness of the pay, from which circumstances one may, I think, infer two things. First they are aware of the necessity of the Measure and secondly, in return for their services, they expect a valuable consideration adequate at least to the profits arising from labour.'

Put into the immortal words of Yorkshire folk the world over, 'Yer can't 'ave summat fer nowt'.

Since it was also harvest time, volunteers were most likely to be found in the fields rather than church halls but one of the most significant reasons for the lack of patriotic zeal from local men was their reluctance to leave their beloved East Riding. Grimston wrote:

'though I doubt not if necessary they will go beyond the limits of the Riding, yet I found them particularly desirous that they should not bind themselves to do it and to please them I was obliged to change the name of the corps from East York Yeomanry Cavalry... to the East Riding Yeomanry Cavalry.'

Once it was settled that men would not serve outside the East Riding boundary, Thomas found he was soon able to recruit the numbers he needed.

He kitted out his men with a leather helmet adorned with a bearskin crest and four small chains to deflect sabre cuts; on the left side was a plume of buff feathers. The scarlet jacket was short, scarlet with buff facings and silver braid, navy blue for officers. The whitened leather crossbelt had a plate engraved with ERYC and the motto *pro aris et focis* (for hearth and home) topped with a crown. White breeches, black riding boots, a sabre and pistol completed the uniform.

Running a cavalry force didn't come cheap. The cost of various items was set out in a letter from the admirably succinctly-named Mr D Egg:

'Sir, I received the favour of yours and the one before wherein you order 42 sabres and 42 pistols and understand you would wish to have some sent as soon as possible which I shall do in a few days and the swords I do furnish are exactly like those used in Elliotts Light Horse and yours shall be the same. The price 19/-s; Pistols - 36/-s the pair; Carbines £2:2:0 each, which is as near as can be what Government pays and everyone else I furnish.'

So the sabres and pistols alone, assuming no fancy additions would cost him around £115, (about £11,000 today).

Pastel portrait of Thomas Grimston reviewing his troops, by Henry Singleton c 1794

Having solved the recruitment and equipping issues the remaining problem for Thomas to solve was the lack of a trumpet with which any decent cavalry unit should be furnished. However, his brother-in-law Richard Ledgard came to his assistance in 1795 and from the accompanying letter, one can only assume that his neighbours would have been pleased to see the back of it:

'... have been blasting all my neighbours this hour past... the cord is crimson and buff, very neat... the price is 3½ guineas, ½ guinea the string, together 4 guineas. What a tremendous sound they produce. It puts me in mind of what we are to expect at our latter end.'

By the turn of the century the Holderness coast swarmed with volunteer corps and they provided much needed support to the regular forces and the militia but the signing of the peace preliminaries in October 1801 reduced the need for such strength and vigilance and many of the volunteer units and militia, including Grimston's Yeomanry, were disbanded or stood down. This was premature however and in May the following year the war was recommenced and Thomas Grimston's yeomanry rode again up and down the Holderness coast.

In June that year, the yeomanry were on duty in Bridlington and were clearly quite hospitable towards civilians although, as this brief diary entry from a Mr Dunn of Patrington shows, perhaps catering was not all it should have been or there again, perhaps it was too good and plentiful:

'5th June - Took chaise for Bridlington to see Grimston Troop.
6th June - went to see the troops at exercise. Came on to rain. Dined with the officers in the Mess.
7th June - very ill until noon.'

The 1807 Local Militia Act saw the end of many of the volunteer forces as it dealt somewhat unfairly with them by incorporating a provision that any man who showed he was an effective member of a volunteer or yeomanry corps and undertook to serve at his own expense, without pay of allowances, nevertheless had to pay a fee to continue to serve. The fee was the equivalent of half the fine paid by those wishing to avoid military service altogether. Whilst many men would have continued to serve without pay and provide their own uniform and weapons, they could not afford to pay the fee in addition, just to remain in the unit. Needless to say, Thomas Grimston's Yeoman Cavalry managed to survive as a unit for a few more years until galloping into the sunset in 1814.

THE SOUNDS OF WAR

The outbreak of the First World War saw the East Yorkshire coast bristling with defences partly aimed at frustrating any attempts to land on the open Holderness beaches and partly to ensure the defence of the busy port of Hull. Military camps sprouted up along the coast and a temporary airfield developed near Withernsea.

The quiet village of Kilnsea was invaded by the military who built Fort Godwin there and what is now the wild nature reserve of Spurn Point was armed with three gun batteries and a signal station. All ships approaching the coast and the Humber estuary used a combination of lights, pennants and sound to show they were friendly. A railway was built to link the installations on Spurn with the forts at Kilnsea.

Perhaps the most intriguing military installation was that of a sound mirror – a huge concave concrete dish designed to pick up the sound of incoming enemy aircraft flying over the North Sea. The sound waves from slow flying aircraft, in Kilnsea's case Zeppelins, were captured and picked up by microphone allowing aircraft to be detected some distance away. Eventually, it was superseded by its big brother radar. The Kilnsea mirror is around 4.5 metres high and provided three or four minutes of extra warning before the attack. How effective it was is debatable. Certainly it and all the military defences on the coast were unable to fend off a Zeppelin attack in 1915 when it offloaded its bombs on the ports of Hull and Grimsby further down the coast, with 60 casualties recorded.

Today much of the First World War installations have tumbled down the cliffs onto the beaches below. However the Kilnsea Sound mirror is now a monument protected by English Heritage.

The Ruins of Fort Godwin

The Kilnsea Sound Mirror

Chapter Seven
I Do Like to be Beside the Seaside

LET MODESTY AND DECORUM BE THE WATCHWORDS

STUDY AT A QUIET FRENCH WATERING-PLACE.

" NOW, THEN, MOSSOO, YOUR FORM IS OF THE MANLIEST BEAUTY, AND YOU ARE ALTOGETHER A MOST ATTRACTIVE OBJECT ; BUT YOU'VE STOOD THERE LONG ENOUGH. SO JUMP IN AND HAVE DONE WITH IT ! "

Study at a quiet French watering place by George du Maurier, *Punch* 1877

If you were a member of a well-heeled 18th century family in Yorkshire you may have followed the advice of Dr Richard Russell and headed for the Holderness coast for a restorative spell of sea bathing. If you were a healthy male you would take a five minute dip but the weaker sex, the feeble and children were prescribed three two-minute dips, three times a week.

When the cold grey waters of the North Sea had frozen you senseless you might have followed up your dip with a nauseous gulp of seawater or sampled the local chalybeate (mineral) spring water.

To preserve modesty and decorum horse drawn bathing machines were provided for hire – mobile changing rooms that were hauled into the sea whilst within, ladies could shed the encumbrances of petticoats and pantaloons for a shift or bathing dress. The advent of the Miss Wet T-shirt competition was still some couple of hundred years off so bathing dresses were often made of a heavy material such as flannel or canvas, which ballooned out when wet to conceal a fair lady's form and figure. Once suitably enveloped, the intrepid bather would emerge straight into the sea for the prescribed dose of three total immersions. She could then retire to the shelter of the bathing machine, modesty intact, to dry off and dress.

However, in this part of the world, the male of the species was permitted more licence and allowed to disport himself in his birthday suit provided he hired a boat, went off shore a little and dropped discreetly over the side. Those of a more modest disposition could cover the dangly bits with a pair of drawers.

By the end of the 18th century sea bathing had taken off and even received the royal seal of approval from George III who being somewhat 'nesh' (that is, something of a wimp), gave it a go in the soft southern waters off Weymouth.

Eventually, Victorian sensibilities took over, demanding more male modesty. Naked bathing was banned around 1861-2; men and women bathers were to be kept 60 feet apart (presumably so as not to shock or over-stimulate the weaker sex) and proprietors of bathing huts were required to provide suitable bathing attire for their clientele. Those who persisted in the pernicious practice of skinny-dipping were punished – like George Large who was discovered, all rosy pink and starkers, bathing in the sea at Hornsea in 1902. He was arrested and fined three shillings plus costs.

Bathing machines arrived in Hornsea around the beginning of the 19th century and the Marine Hotel opened its doors to genteel visitors – none of the great unwashed wanted here! Further down the coast Aldbrough, not to be outdone, did likewise and catered for its visitors' needs at the Talbot Hotel and the Spa Inn.

In Bridlington, the citizens stole a march on their coastal neighbours and provided both warm and cold sea water baths which gave the faint of heart all the benefits of sea bathing without actually having to brave the ocean itself.

Of course the arrival of the railway to the Holderness coast spoilt it all for the wealthy sea-bathers bringing, as it did, crowded carriages of escapees from daily drudgery all seeking 'A Good Time'. What was an exclusive practice became commonplace fun and games, requiring the rich to seek playgrounds elsewhere wherein to seek cures for their numerous ills – real or imaginary.

Hence, depending on the viewpoint, it was the best of times or it was the worst of times. The coming of the railways to previously undistinguished coastal towns and villages provided a wonderful opportunity for such places to develop into that bastion of Britishness – the seaside resort together with its promenade, boarding houses, battle-axe landladies and sand in the unmentionables.

TEMPTED BY A QUADRILLE BAND AND CHEAP SEASON TICKETS

Bridlington was the first of the Holderness resort trio to be connected to the wider world by rail in 1846, followed by Withernsea in 1854 and ten years later by Hornsea – whose good townsfolk were wracked by doubts as to the desirability of opening the little town up to what might turn out to be the *hoi polloi.*

Withernsea started life as a small insignificant village on the southern part of the Holderness coast. Already a victim of coastal erosion, (old Withernsea lay under the waves out at sea) new Withernsea (population 109) knew a thing or two about reinventing itself and was determined to make its way in the world.

When the railway came to Holderness, the village took its chance, which arrived in 1854 in the shape of the Hull and Holderness Railway and masterminded by a Hull merchant, Anthony Bannister. Folk dreamed of developing Withernsea as a resort to rival Scarborough further north up the coast. Further ambition blossomed with the happy thought that a significant east-west trade route between Withernsea and Liverpool could be developed – although to be fair this nearly did happen when the Hull and Holderness line was taken over by the North Eastern Railway.

The development of Withernsea followed hot on the tracks of the trains. A hotel and terraced housing sprang up like mushrooms, to be followed by chapels, shops, schools, refreshment houses and public houses. The more well-heeled who moved into Withernsea in search of another pot of gold built themselves large houses from where they conducted their domestic and business affairs.

In 1861, Walter White on his travels around Yorkshire, described Withernsea thus:

'a small watering-place, the terminus of the Hull and Holderness Railway, to which the natives of the melancholy town [his description of Hull] *betake themselves for health and recreation, tempted by a quadrille band and cheap season-tickets.'*

The initial development stuttered somewhat and it was not until someone had the bright idea of building a pier and providing entertainment for the visitors that things began to look up. The Withernsea Pier, Promenade, Gas & General Improvement Company was formed in 1872. Despite the burden of its name, the good men of the company readily sprang into action commissioning a new sea wall and a grand promenade stretching right across the front of what by now, in 1875, qualified as a town. Two years later the desired pier, designed by Thomas Cargill, struck boldly out to sea for a length of 1,200 feet and at a cost of £1 per foot.

The final act in this building frenzy was to build a lighthouse in an effort to reduce the number of shipwrecks that happened off Withernsea. At this point on the coast, ships could not see the lights of either Spurn to the south or Flamborough to the north, and hence lost their way. Rather unusually, it was sited about a quarter of a mile inland with a mere and sandiness between it and the sea. Later more housing was erected around it, until today it appears stranded in the middle of the town.

The pier enjoyed a somewhat truncated history, being regularly assaulted by wayward shipping. In 1880 the coal barge *Saffron* collided with the central section of the pier. Although the section was replaced, with timber substituted for the original metal work, a storm took away the end section of the structure two years later. The good folk of Withernsea didn't have much luck with their pier because in 1890 a fishing smack – the *Genesta* – crashed into it making a serious mess of more than half the remaining structure. Roll the calendar forward another three years and the vessel *Henry Marr* and another unknown ship both collided with the pier until, of the original 1,200 feet, only 50 feet remained. This length was demolished but the entrance to the pier, said to be modelled on Conwy Castle, was left standing as a monument to ambition and ill-fortune.

Withernsea Pier Head

A Tale of Two Piers

Not only did the emerging seaside towns vie with each other for a greater share of the holidaymakers but some of their citizens took up the cudgels with each other – business is business after all.

In Hornsea, the leading light, 'King Hornsea' was a gentleman called Joseph Armytage Wade. He was a businessman, a significant local employer, had all ten fingers in 20 local pies and was liberally endowed with all the necessary characteristics, being bombastic, over-bearing, and self-righteous, so rightly earning the title of town prat. He decided that what Hornsea really needed to attract visitors was a pier and to this end, in 1865, he formed a company and obtained the necessary permissions to build one. He got as far as driving ten piles into the sand of the proposed site and then stopped. The ten piles, known locally as the ten virgins stood, as all good virgins should, untouched, and as such for the next ten years.

Fast forward ten years and enter into the lists one Pierre Henri Martin du Gillon, a foreigner and – *sacre bleu!* – a Frenchman to boot. Du Gillon bought a well-situated lump of land and drew up the most visionary and spectacular plans for 'his' pier – to be known as the South Pier. He didn't just want a plank platform sticking out to sea – no, his plans included housing, an hotel, an aquarium and gardens, all to be protected by a huge sea wall. Yet there was more. He cleverly planned a quay for fishing boats such as the herring fleets where they could land their catches. The quay would be linked by a tramway to the railway station and from thence to the fish markets at Hull. The plan outshone anything Mr Wade had ever come up with. The townsfolk rubbed their hands with glee in anticipation of making sure that any forthcoming wealth stuck firmly to them!

There was just one teensy-weensy fly in the ointment – du Gillon needed a narrow strip of land to link the proposed site to the railway station – land owned and suddenly cherished by Mr Wade. Discussions were opened and, cordiality being the *plat du jour,* our Frenchman came away from the discussions under the impression he had reached an agreement with Wade for the sale of the strip of land. Du Gillon drew up the agreement but Wade refused to sign it.

From that point on it was shovels at ten paces and the dispute went on to reach into the highest courts in the land. Thinly veiled allegations, not so veiled insults, letters to the press – Wade threw the works at du Gillon and yet, sensing he had the townsfolk and two powerful local landowners behind him, du Gillon pressed on. Wade's current actions and earlier inaction stirred up the town against him but he was nothing if not a doughty and dirty fighter.

When Du Gillon applied for a compulsory purchase order for the land, the local Board of Health was consulted. Wade, as Chair of the Board, whilst appearing to support du Gillon's plans pointed out (no doubt in feigned innocent concern) that the strip of land impinged on local sewage arrangements and the board would need to think very carefully before supporting the purchase order in case it affected the town's health interests. It was all a pile of poo but it threw yet another shovel in the works for du Gillon. But he rode his luck and, buoyed on by local support, applied for permission to build his South Pier. Nothing daunted Wade hit back by renewing his application to build his pier – the North Pier. Battle was joined. Finally both men appeared before a House of Commons Select Committee whose chairman ruled thus, *'Each of you agree to the construction of the other's pier or permission will only be granted for the building of one pier.'*

In the end they agreed the compromise and little Hornsea was to become a two pier town.

Du Gillon was first out of the stalls in the building stakes but his scheme was doomed to failure. His capital had been eaten up with legal costs and he discovered that, in Hornsea, converting public support into public funds was akin to the water and wine miracle and certainly beyond his talents. He ran out of cash to splash and finally the weather did for him. A fierce storm blew up destroying his equipment and machinery overnight. He wound up his pier company and left Hornsea, never to return.

His rival, after some serious gloating, fared little better when it came to finances and although the North Pier was finished for the summer of 1880, one of the construction companies to whom Wade owed money took out a restraining order preventing Wade from taking possession of it. So whilst Hornsea had a pier stretching out to sea, it couldn't actually be used. Later that autumn, during a violent storm, the brig the *Earl of Derby* lost her sails and was driven inexorably onto the newly built pier. The omens were not auspicious.

Eventually in the summer of 1881 Wade's North Pier opened but never really attracted the paying punters and the locals were not overly enthusiastic either – especially about having to pay to go on it, some getting into the habit of breaking in after hours. Wade died in 1896 and his pier just outlasted him before being demolished in 1897. Thus ends the tale of two piers.

Hornsea promenade and pier remains, pre-1906

THAT'S THE WAY TO DO IT

However invigorating and bracing the sea air, a walk up and down the pier or on the sands was not enough for the new trippers – they wanted entertainment. Along the Holderness coastline residents of Bridlington, Hornsea, and Withernsea put on their thinking caps and added visitor attractions to entice these trippers to part company with their hard-earned 'brass'. Donkey rides, Punch and Judy shows, pierrots, tea dances and palm court orchestras all strived to keep these new invaders happy.

Donkeys made an early appearance on the beaches. At Bridlington donkeys used to draw carts for cockle gatherers. Around 1895/6, after a good wash and brush up, they made their debut as tourist carriers. They also became an important prop in the postcard and photography business when shops such as Snaps created the donkey studio portrait as a keepsake. Toddlers (and larger specimens!) would be perched on a donkey standing in front of an improbable backdrop (they rarely used the real surroundings) whilst the photograph was taken. It must be said that, from those photos which survived, it is the donkey that tends to produce the most winsome portrait.

Hornsea and Withernsea had their own donkey troops too which seemed to attract good business, so much so that residents in Hornsea complained bitterly about the donkey races held up and down the local streets at the beginning of the 20th century.

Despite the lure of these myriad attractions there can have been none so amazing and outlandish than Colonel Harrison's Pygmy Troop who made appearances in Hornsea and Withernsea in the early years of the 20th century. Whilst the whole idea is totally out of tune with today's attitudes and culture, back then curiosity, ignorance, imperialism and a general sense of superiority over the rest of the world all played a part in bringing this type of entertainment to England. Here's the story...

In 1904 Colonel James Harrison of Brandesburton Hall in the East Riding of Yorkshire was travelling through the Congo river basin. This was not as odd as you might surmise since he was not only a soldier but also an explorer and big game hunter. Travelling in darkest Africa is what explorers are supposed to do.

There in the remoteness of the Congo he made the acquaintance of the Pygmy tribe of the Ituri forest. No doubt after a deal of huffing and puffing he persuaded six of his new *'little pygmie friends'* to return to England with him. So it was that Bokane, Quarke, Mogonga, Matuka, Amurape and Masutiminga arrived in 1905, to take London by storm. Appearances at the London Hippodrome, Olympia and even the staid old House of Commons were followed by a tour of the whole country when all and sundry could pay up and gawk at them.

In their free time the group stayed at Brandesburton Hall and went hunting in the parkland there. They made appearances at various venues in East Yorkshire including the coastal resorts of Hornsea and Withernsea where they met with a great deal of interest.

During their stay a record was made of them speaking their native language – although what they made of the denizens of these shores is not on record. All six survived their English tour and returned to their homeland in 1907/8.

Chapter Eight
The Lost Villages

One constant in the history of this coast is the sea's insatiable appetite for gobbling up the land. Some estimates suggest that since the Norman Conquest in 1066 the sea has taken back to itself two miles of coastline. In that time people living on this coast have learned to adapt or go under. Villages such as Aldbrough, Withernsea and Kilnsea reinvented themselves by moving further inland and some that were once inland settlements such as Skipsea and Hornsea are now perched on the coast.

Nearly 30 villages have disappeared altogether beneath the waves and today their names form a sad litany, recited only in local history books and gazettes or recorded in place names. For what information there is about the lost communities we are indebted to the two Thomases: Thomas Burton, Abbot of Meaux Abbey who wrote the *Chronicles of the Abbey* and Thomas Sheppard who published *The Lost Towns of the Yorkshire Coast* in 1912. It is to Sheppard that we are indebted for the original map of the lost settlements.

So, in tribute to his indefatigable wanderings up and down the coast and the wealth of measurements and distances from the sea with which he spoils us, I am going to attempt to emulate him (without the measurements or indeed the erudite turn of phrase), starting at the northern end of the coast.

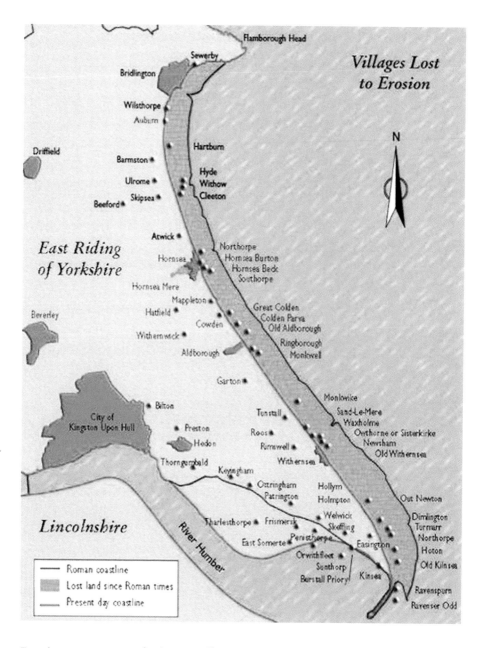

Erosion map and lost villages, adapted from Thomas Sheppard's *The Lost Towns of the Yorkshire Coast,* 1912

Wilsthorpe village had been lost to the sea certainly by the early 20th century with just one house remaining and a few years later, just a handful of bricks on the beach. Today Wilsthorpe Sands is all that is left to commemorate the village; a quiet spot with sand dunes and low cliffs, popular with fishermen and dog walkers.

By the mid-19th century most of Auburn had disappeared under the waves and, at high spring tides would be lying under 16 feet of water. In 1781 the chapel in the village was dismantled. A Bulmer's gazette entry for 1870-72 tells us that 16 people still clung to a living there and that there were but two houses.

The last building standing was Auburn House and once the sea reached this point, according to Sheppard it *'seemed to stay its work'* and the house was untouched and still habitable. Here is how our inimitable author and hiker Walter White, writing in the mid-19th century, described his first view of the remains of Auburn:

'... you see a poor weather-beaten cottage on the top of the cliff, and so close to the edge that the eastern wall forms but one perpendicular line with the cliff itself. You can hardly help fancying that it will fall at any moment, even while you are looking; but so it has stood for many years; a fact the more remarkable, as in this place the cliff projects as if in defiance of the ruthless waters. Look at the old maps, and you will read: "Here Auburn washed away by the sea;" and the lone house remains a melancholy yet suggestive monument of geological change.'

A Month in Yorkshire, 1861

Hartburn and Winkton were lost back in medieval times. Both settlements were originally part of the parish of Barmston.

Hartburn was situated in the north-east corner of the parish next to the Earl's Dike one of the parish boundaries. The name is Anglo-Saxon meaning the 'Hart's stream'. Meaux Abbey held land in the village and bemoaned its drowning in the sea with the consequent loss of tithes. Friars from Bridlington Priory used the village water mill, situated on the Dike. Despite the drainage schemes developed in the parish some parts remained as carrs – marshy areas, often wooded with alder and hazel. Turbary – the right to cut peat – was a valuable concession to the ordinary folk living there in the settlement in the late 12th century. By the 15th century the settlement was deserted; the rude dwellings decayed and fell as gradually the sea took the land back to itself.

Winkton, or Winchetone as the Domesday Book dubbed it, followed the same fate as Hartburn. Its actual site is not known but it is thought that it lay in the northern part of Barmston parish. Possibly the name comes from Anglo-Saxon meaning 'Wineca's Farm'. In the 12th century most of the land was held by the Monceaux family, passing through deaths and marriages to the Boynton family of Burton Agnes.

Again, the church held land within the settlement, notably Thornton Abbey in Lincolnshire. In the mid-14th century the abbey owned a house there as well as around four acres of land. As in Hartburn, the villagers enjoyed rights of turbary. Apparently inhabited in the 15th century it was abandoned soon after.

Alongside this cluster of lost villages lies the village of Barmston itself, located east of the main A165 to Bridlington and quietly losing land to the sea every year at an average rate of 1metre.

HYDE, WITHOW AND CLEETON

Moving further south down the coast we find the parish and village of Skipsea and the probable sites of the lost villages of Hyde, Withow and Cleeton. Of these three, Cleeton was the largest and originally more important than neighbouring Skipsea. Cleeton is sometimes translated as Clay town. It appears to have lost its inhabitants certainly by the 19th century, although remembered in place names and possibly in Clayton Farm.

Hyde or Hythe meaning a 'port' or 'haven' in Saxon was to be found east of Skipsea but now lies far out to sea. By the time of Edward III (14th century) the sea was eating away at the village and the king received a petition for a reduction in its tax assessment as a consequence of much of the village being lost. Meaux Abbey also lost tithes from fishing from Hyde and records the place as being totally destroyed by 1396.

Withow, originally part of Cleeton township, was built on the shore of an ancient mere or lake where, in the 19th century the remains of an elk were found. The eastern remnant of the lake is now a site of special scientific interest known as Withow Hole or Skipsea Withow. The sea continues its depredations and in 2012 the cliff top path between Withow and Skipsea was closed due to erosion.

Skipsea, like its neighbour Barmston, has suffered much loss through erosion. Once an inland settlement established on the same lake as Withow, the lake was drained and so much land lost to the sea that Skipsea turned into a small seaside village. At one point in 1891 the village was about three-quarters of a mile from the sea; today the sea laps at the doorsteps of the chalets and caravans sited on the parks.

NORTHORPE TO HORNSEA BURTON

Moving south further down the coast between the little village of Atwick and the market town of Hornsea, we should find

Northorpe. It did not feature in the Domesday Book but it is mentioned as a settlement in later documents. In 1377 there were just seven poll tax payers living there; by the end of the 15th century this number had doubled and yet in a further 100 years there was just a ruined house and the whole place was consigned to oblivion. Possibly it was a dormitory settlement for its big brother Hornsea just down the road which was expanding rapidly. There is a Northorpe Farm today but no evidence of the settlement itself. One school of thought is that rather than being a quarter of a mile to the north of Hornsea it may have been further east and been taken by the sea.

Either side of Hornsea there are two settlements that the sea most definitely did gobble up. Hornsea Beck to the north/east of Hornsea was a small fishing village and port with a pier for loading and unloading goods for which tolls could be charged. It comes to our attention in 1228 when a dispute between the beneficiaries of a will – Meaux Abbey, St Mary's Abbey and the Lord of the Manor – occurred. The outcome of the dispute was that St Mary's Abbey agreed to shoulder the cost of the upkeep of the pier and harbour at the settlement.

The folk who lived in Hornsea Beck were mainly fishermen with a few merchants and other traders thrown in for good measure. It was clearly a thriving community – the Poll Tax lists of 1377 show that there were 264 potential tax payers making it a settlement of comparable size to Hornsea.

The sea began to fight back during the 15th century when the population had diminished by half. At an Inquiry in the early 17th century evidence was produced to show, *'we find decayed by the flowing of the sea, in Hornsea Beck, since 1546, 39 houses and as many closes adjoining.'*

Although the pier still survived it did not last much longer being washed away in the mid-17th century. By the end of that century just a few houses remained and the last we hear of

Hornsea Beck was that in 1785 the house of one Robin Maudsley was washed away. A map by John Tuke issued a year later shows a poignant cross offshore marking the site of Hornsea Beck.

The second settlement that succumbed to the sea was Hornsea Burton, situated to the south of Hornsea. It was originally held by the Lord of Holderness, Drogo but was given later to St Mary's Abbey, York. Meaux Abbey also obtained land and property within the town including rights to fish in Hornsea Mere. The town regularly lost land to the sea and the population upped sticks and moved elsewhere. By 1663 although the open fields had been enclosed only eight houses remained and four years later the sea had swallowed them up. Whatever the sea left of Hornsea Burton was soon annexed by Hornsea itself and today it is remembered in road names.

Sandwiched in between these two lost settlements, the little town of Hornsea survives, mainly as a commuter town to Hull and Beverley or as a place to retire. Once it was said to be about ten miles from the sea; now the sea laps hungrily on the doorstep only stymied by the presence of coastal defences erected in the early 1900s.

THE COWDENS

Moving on southwards we pass through Mappleton to the next two lost settlements, Great Colden (Cowden) and Colden Parva. Strictly speaking these two settlements combined and re-located further inland. However they both lost so much land that they fit better in the lost villages category.

The original village of Great Colden lies about 140 metres out at sea. The main street and other roads, fields, manor house, chapel and pub all disappeared over time, mostly in the late 19th and early 20th centuries. The Cross Keys public house, present in the village at least since 1822 was rebuilt in 1943 further inland and now rejoices in the name the Blue Boar. The village features in the Domesday Book as Coledun and was part of the holdings of the Archbishop of York.

Colden Parva (Little Cowden) had seven houses in 1401 and during early enclosure of its land 24 people were evicted. In 1690 the church was swept to the sea and the village was largely abandoned.

Today, both Cowdens have merged to form a settlement further inland of which a large caravan site forms the main part.

OLD ALDBROUGH TO WITHERNSEA

South from Cowden, Old Aldbrough is the next lost village. As with the Cowdens, today's Aldbrough represents a migration inland and the original settlement built around a Saxon church lies far out to sea. It is said that on stormy nights the bells of Old Aldbrough can still be heard to toll.

Between Aldbrough and Tunstall we find Ringborough, Monkwell and Monkwike... or rather we do not find them because all three, despite being recorded in the Domesday Book (when Monkwike seemed to be a settlement of some size and importance) are gone.

The hamlet of Ringborough is a little unusual in that for a time it was given a second lease of life. The original settlement had fallen into the sea, all bar a single farm, by the middle of the 19th century. However, during the Second World War the remaining land was commandeered for a military installation. There were gun emplacements, munitions trackways, bunkers and lookout posts and for a while life returned. Today, the sea steadily eats away at the cliffs and the Second World War archaeology is disappearing over the edge much in the same way as the original village.

From Ringborough southwards another cluster of villages slowly vanished, Sand le Mere, Waxholme and Newsham.

Thomas Sheppard writing in 1912 describes Sand le Mere as, *'destitute of all attractions... except a wide and solitary expanse of the German Ocean'.*

At one time there was a Watch House at Waxholme for the Preventative men to keep an eye out for smugglers and signs of smuggling. It was then taken over by the coastguard but by the early 20th century was gone. There is also some reference to a small chapel there but details are sadly lacking. As far as Newsham is concerned the Domesday Book tells us it was once a large settlement with some 600 acres but by the late 18th century all trace and memory of it had vanished, which brings us to the village of Owthorne (sometimes called Seathorne) and what is left of it is now a part of modern day Withernsea.

OWTHORNE AND THE SISTER CHURCHES

The story of Owthorne and its church comes to the fore to illustrate the almost surreal events that occasionally happened when the sea claimed the land.

Owthorne was a small village just north of Withernsea. In the centre of the village was the church, known as one of the Sister Churches. The story is told that two sisters owned the manors of Owthorne and Withernsea. Since the two manors ran side by side, they decided to build a church where their tenants could worship. The site of Owthorne Church was agreed upon and building commenced. It was only when the church had reached a certain height that discord between the sisters set in. One wished to adorn the church with a tower and the other to ornament it with a spire.

Square or Pointy? That is the question... In the end, possibly at prompting by vested interests, the sisters decided that they would each build a church – one in Withernsea and one in Owthorne – in the design to which they each aspired. For ever after, the churches were known as the Sister Churches but no spire ever graced either church.

Whatever the circumstances of its origin, there is no doubt that the church at Owthorne was constantly under threat from the sea. Originally sited in the centre of the village, as the sea ate away the foot of the cliffs the church at the top became a cliff-hanger, *'standing like a solitary beacon on the verge of the cliff'*.

By 1786 the sea began its work on the churchyard and the church itself was only 12 yards from the cliff. The villagers and their vicar made plans. In 1793 the chancel was demolished and six years later the church was partially demolished. It was not until a particularly violent storm in the early years of the 19th century that the remains of the church fell with a crash into the sea. Whitened bones and coffins landed on the beach and, it is said, that the villagers meandered sorrowfully amongst these relics, even (allegedly) recognising some of their erstwhile buddies although quite how one recognises a skeleton is a trifle difficult to imagine. It took 15 days of grisly work to collect up the relics, hopefully matching owners and bones correctly, before taking them for reburial to a new churchyard at Rimswell.

In 50 years the villagers of Owthorne saw the church and churchyard, vicarage, houses and streets disappear over the cliffs until almost nothing of their village remained. The second church in Withernsea fell into ruins by the late 19th century and was replaced by the parish church of St Nicholas.

Gravestones – Rimswell Churchyard

OLD WITHERNSEA TO KILNSEA

The final cluster of lost villages takes us from Old Withernsea through Turmarr, Hoton, Northorpe, Dimlington, Old Kilnsea and Ravenser. Of these, we know little of the first three. Turmarr is remembered in the place name, Turmarr Bottom; Hoton and Northorpe disappeared in the late 14th century. These villages have taken their histories with them.

Dimlington is another village offered a second lease of life. It was located on the highest point of the Holderness coast but by the 14th century the sea had washed away most of the village, including its watch beacon and an old chapel that served as a landfall point for ships out at sea. Today's Dimlington is part of the Easington Gas Terminal bringing North Sea gas ashore and still fighting against erosion by the sea.

Old Kilnsea (called Chilnesse in the Domesday Book) was then several miles inland and established on a hill. Houses and cottages with gardens were clustered around the Medieval church; there was a village pond and green as well as numerous small fields. On the village green a large stone cross formed a landmark in the village, which was originally taken from the ancient and lost town of Ravenser where it had been erected to commemorate the landing of Henry VI in 1399. It was removed to Old Kilnsea when the sea swallowed up Ravenser. Eventually though, the sea worked its mischief in Kilnsea and the cross was removed altogether to safer ground.

By the early 19th century the village was under attack; in 1822 it comprised the church and around 30 houses; 30 years later only a handful of houses and the foundations of the church remained and by 1912 all had gone.

In 1824 the chancel went over the cliff and a couple of years later a huge storm took the north wall, pillars, arches, pulpit, reading desk and books right over the cliff *'with a tremendous crash'*. The tower held out for another couple of years before finally following the rest of the church over the cliff.

After the loss of the church, Abbot Geoffrey de Sawtry describes Kilnsea religious observance thus:

'... This is therefore another churchless village; but having a population of nearly two hundred, they have set apart a room for divine service, in which it is performed every third Sunday, weather permitting; otherwise, it is reported, the worthy pastor, feeling for his flock, grants them an indulgence to remain indoors and takes the same himself.'

The church bell was suspended from a beam in a stack yard and struck by throwing stones at it to call the faithful to their improvised place of worship.

Even though Kilnsea has resettled itself to the west it is still being chased further inland by the sea.

However, perhaps the most famous disappearing act was that of Ravenser Odd, situated right on the southern tip of the coast and now somewhere in the North Sea, to the east of Spurn Point. We have the helpful chronicler of Meaux Abbey to thank for much of the detail which helps to piece together the colourful history of this port.

RAVENSER ODD – THE TOWN UNDER THE SEA

'The town of Ravenser Odd was an extremely famous borough, devoted to merchandise with many fisheries and the most abundantly provided with ships and burgesses of all the boroughs of that coast. But yet, by all its wicked deeds and especially wrong-doings on the sea, and by its evil actions and predations, it provoked the vengeance of God upon itself beyond measure.'

Such was the verdict of the chronicler writing in the mid-14th century when documenting the destruction of the town.

The monk's records reveal that the town began life as a sandbank, probably an island, thrown up by the tides and currents between the River Humber and the North Sea. Located off the tip of Spurn Point and about a mile off the Holderness coast, at some point it became accessible from the mainland via a sandy path strewn with yellow stones.

The sandbank grew and was initially inhabited by a handful of enterprising souls selling provisions to passing ships. Around 1235 the Count and Countess of Aumale whose fiefdom embraced Holderness, recognised the strategic possibilities of the site and started to build the town. A few years later the monks of Meaux Abbey got in on the act and acquired buildings there for storing fish and other provisions.

The town prospered. Its position between the Humber and the North Sea was perfect for fishing, trading and servicing shipping. Perhaps being at the outer reaches of the Holderness coast and away from any regular attention of the law, the men of Ravenser Odd were able to develop their own approach to trade by intercepting merchant ships and 'persuading' them to berth at their port rather than at Hull or Grimsby. This practice, called forestalling, became a bone of contention with the merchants of Hull and Grimsby who saw their own trade suffer. In 1290 the king instituted an Inquiry into the deeds of the Ravenser Odd men. Grimsby merchants asserted that the Ravenser Odd men would:

'go out with their boats where there are ships carrying merchandise and intending to come to Grimsby with their merchandise. Said men hinder those ships and lead them to Ravenser Odd harbour by force when they cannot persuade them amicably.'

They also accused the Ravenser Odd men of giving false information to merchants to entice them away from Grimsby. They asserted that on several occasions the Ravenser Odd men spread the word that merchants would get a lower price for their goods at Grimsby than they would in their port when, in fact, the opposite was true. The men of Ravenser Odd made a swift counter claim, levelling the same accusations at the Grimsby men. It was a case of the pot calling the kettle. The men of Ravenser Odd triumphed with all charges not proven.

In 1293, on the death of the Countess of Aumale, Ravenser Odd passed to the King, Edward 1. The town flourished with more than 100 houses, warehouses, quays and other port buildings. It was granted borough status in 1298/9 for which the then huge sum of £300 was paid. It is in keeping with the spirit of the town that little of the money was actually handed over.

With its new status the town gained perks and freedoms including a warden, a coroner, a set of gallows and, most important of all, the right to collect a very wide range of tolls and taxes. Yet there is still some evidence that the Ravenser Odd men found it hard to shake off old ways and become model citizens. Around 1300 two Norwegian merchants petitioned the English king claiming that when their ship was driven ashore off Ravenser Odd, *'men came from there with force and arms and stole our ship and goods'*. The petition ends with a plaintive request for remedy and compensation for their goods as they *'have nothing from which to live'*.

Under the king's patronage, whatever piracy and misdemeanours were committed were ignored and the town grew in importance, wealth and prosperity. The town was represented by two MPs in the Model Parliament of the time and supported the king in the wars against the Scots by providing ships, provisions, arms and men.

However, by the middle of the century it became clear that the golden years of Ravenser Odd were drawing to a close. Merchants started to move away as the flooding by the sea became more regular and more serious. There were a number of petitions made for the lowering of taxes because buildings and land had been washed away.

In 1355 flooding damaged the chapel in the town exposing bones and corpses. These were removed to Easington for reburial. The chapel itself was ultimately washed away but not before some of the townsfolk looted many of its artefacts leaving little for the monks to gather up.

The Meaux chronicler described how, on one occasion, both the Humber and the sea flooded the town *'to a height exceeding the existing buildings'* and the few remaining townsfolk, surrounded on all sides by the floodwaters *'preserved themselves at that time from destruction, flocking together and imploring grace'.*

For a while after the town was abandoned it became, perhaps unsurprisingly, a pirates' lair until the *coup de grace* was applied in 1362. In January of that year a south-westerly gale stormed across the UK reaching Yorkshire's east coast around the middle of the month. This storm, known as the Great Drowning of Men, raged across the North Sea and, combined with unusually high tides, produced a storm surge that swept the last stones of Ravenser Odd back to the sea. The town founded on a sandbank vanished without trace.

Looking across the Binks, east of Spurn towards the possible site of Ravenser Odd

Epilogue

It is difficult to leave the past without at least some thoughts turning to what will happen in the future. East Yorkshire Council to whom falls the unenviable task of making decisions about the future of the Holderness coast, has developed a Shoreline Management Plan in conjunction with other interested parties.

In a nutshell some parts of the coast are and will continue to be defended. These include Bridlington, Hornsea and Withernsea as the most populated areas, together with Mappleton, Easington and Dimlington cliffs and Barmston Drain and Tunstall. These are important areas in relation to roads, industry and flood management.

Other areas will be left for nature to take its course. Erosion has been a constant along the coast and has shaped and will reshape the coastline. It is neither feasible nor affordable to defend the whole coastline from erosion.

That is why collecting and recording the history of this moody coast is so important before it disappears. The work of local history groups and local museums is vital in this and I hope that this mite will make a contribution.

Bibliography

A History of the County of York, Vol 3; British History Online (www.british-history.ac.uk)

A Tour Through the Whole Island of Great Britain by Daniel Defoe, 1724-26. Now available published by Penguin

Bygone Yorkshire, edited by William Andrews; A Brown and Son, 1892 (available through www.openlibrary.org)

Folklore of East Yorkshire by John Nicholson; A Brown and Son, 1890 (www.openlibrary.org)

A Month in Yorkshire by Walter White; Chapman & Hall,1861 (available through Project Gutenberg; www.gutenberg.org)

History and Antiquities of the Seigniory of Holderness in the East Riding of the County of York by George Poulson and Thomas Topping, 1840 (www.openlibrary.org)

King's Cutters and Smugglers 1700-1855 by E Keble Chatterton; George Allen & Co, 1912 (www.gutenberg.org)

The Birds of Yorkshire by T H Nelson; A Brown & Sons, 1907 (www.openlibrary.org)

Essays in Natural History, Vol 1 by Charles Waterton; Longman, Brown, Green & Longmans, 1846

The Lost Towns of the Yorkshire Coast by Thomas Sheppard; A Brown & Sons, 1912 (www.openlibrary.org)

Further useful websites

Wikipedia – always a good starting point

www.hidden-holderness.org.uk

www.plimsoll.org.uk (for the Board of Trade wreck reports)

www.engineering-timelines.com

www.genuki.org.uk

www.cistercians.shef.ac.uk

www.levity.com/alchemy/ripgat1.html

For further information about the Flamborough Lifeboats, enter - The Flamborough Lifeboats website - in your search engine and you will be redirected to the site.

About the Author

As a child Sheila Williams read and read – any books about anything. In the Fifties, her first story, *The Canary,* was published in the school magazine. She just missed out on free love and flower power in the Sixties but made up for it in the following decade when she became part of the self-sufficiency movement. She dragged her husband to a smallholding in the Yorkshire Dales, graduated to a farm and then a divorce.

The Seventies and Eighties were productive writing times for Sheila, with many published articles, bits for BBC Radio, a column in a local newspaper and a two-minute slot every week on Indie radio.

The Nineties saw her lured back into business and with her new partner set up a human resources and training consultancy. During this time she wrote extensively for professional journals.

The new century brought a rash of changes in her life when she moved to the coast, bought and renovated a wreck of a cottage, closed down the consultancy and picked up her pen to resuscitate her writing career. She wrote and published a self-help book, *Time for Your Life,* (available on Amazon) before starting the research and writing of *Close to the Edge.*

Sheila now lives in South-West France where she has started yet another house renovation project and another book.

To contact Sheila: Sheila@writeonthebeach.co.uk